THE STORMS

HAVE ONLY

JUST BEGUN

BECOMING HOUSES WHO WILL STAND IN
THE RELENTLESS STORMS OF THE DECADE

ROB STREETMAN

VIDE

Vide Press
6200 Second Street
Washington D.C. 20011
www.VidePress.com

PB ISBN: 978-1-954618-45-9
e-Book ISBN: 978-1-954618-46-6

Printed in the United States of America

Dedication

To the women and men of God
who have been strong houses of refuge, encouragement,
and wisdom during the storms of my life.

Table of Contents

Preface

Back in 2015, we wrote a small eBook, entitled *A Storm is Coming*, in response to the warnings made by Jonathan Cahn in his book, *The Harbinger* (2012). Cahn suggested an economic storm would occur in America sometime in 2015. Many took steps to protect themselves, mostly in a physical way (i.e., prepping). *A Storm is Coming* encouraged Christians to focus first on their spiritual preparation.

The storm did not occur, at least not with the timing and devastation anticipated. Prophesy can be tricky, particularly when one attempts to include dates. However, God works all things to the good of those who love Him and are called to His purposes (Romans 8:28).

God used *The Harbinger* and *A Storm is Coming* to call many watchmen to their posts. Many Christians began to reassess where they had placed their trust. Each one has since grown in their understanding of God's kingdom and their faith in His working for their good.

And now, here at the beginning of a new decade, the storms have arrived like hurricanes, in the form of a worldwide pandemic, economic recession, and social upheaval. The 2020s promise to be the most chaotic, storm-filled decade our generation has experienced. Will our houses withstand the tumult?

As it was with *A Storm is Coming*, this book is primarily written to Christians who reside in the United States of America. However, storms are everywhere. Where would one go to escape the multi-faceted chaos that threatens the entire world in the coming decade?

Many of our brothers and sisters around the world have been weathering storms for most of their lives (e.g., Christians born into persecution and/or severe poverty). Even in the "free" world, it would be difficult to find a single individual—particularly a Christian—that has not experienced chaos and suffering in some form or another. Frankly, we shouldn't be surprised. Jesus Christ promised tribulation.

> *These things I have spoken to you, that in Me you may have peace. In the world you will have tribulation; but be of good cheer, I have overcome the world (John 16:33).*

Christians are resilient people, and Americans pride themselves in their ability to "weather any storm". But these storms are different. The chaos that began in 2020 will likely continue for most of the coming decade and be uniquely pervasive, fierce, and disruptive.

Those already suffering major storms will not be as shocked and traumatized, becoming sources of encouragement and example to the rest. On the other hand, spiritually unprepared Christians will find their foundations suspect and their houses falling down around them. We hope and pray this book will help mitigate such a catastrophe and better prepare mature Christians to become houses of refuge, encouragement, and spiritual understanding.

Introduction

In early 2015, my father asked me how much stock I was putting into the proposition of God's soon coming judgment on America, as presented in *The Harbinger* (Cahn, 2012). I did not have a strong answer. In essence, I did not know what the Lord would have me believe. So I asked Him.

In short, I received the Lord's affirmation that a storm was indeed coming to America; and, most importantly, that judgment was coming to the church that resides here. The Lord encouraged me to prepare spiritually; and to help others do the same. Helping others manifested itself in a series of articles on the inLight Adventures blog site and a short eBook, *A Storm is Coming*.

In the intervening five years, God has stirred a desire in my heart to become, and help others become, houses who stand in the storms of life—a direct reference to Jesus' warning at the end of the Sermon on the Mount (Matthew 7:24-27). God has promised to give us the desires of our heart (Psalm 37:4). He does that for me by using me as His pen.

The Storms of God's Judgment

It is important to clarify, God never gave me a specific date for His judgment on the church in America. First of all, I am not a prophet. Secondly, God does not judge one moment and stop judging the next. He is always, and will always, be the Judge of all creation—beginning with His people.

The church in America has been in decline for some time now, beginning long before 2015. However, our slide down the slippery slope of carnal compromise has accelerated over the last five years. One must wonder if God has not altogether removed His favor and protection. The social, economic, and political unrest of the coming decade threatens to further fast-track the church's decline—at least as long as she determines to be a compromised subculture to the American way of life.

---

*As we mourn with the families of those twenty-one martyrs, we'd better take this warning seriously as these acts of terror will only spread throughout Europe and the United States. If this concerns you like it does me, share this. **The storm is coming.** Franklin Graham (2015 Facebook post in response to ISIS murder of twenty-one Egyptian Christians)*

During this same time, the ISIS terrorist organization decimated much of Middle Eastern Christianity. The storms we are facing threaten to do the same here in America. The Church in America faces a crossroads described by Romans 12:2.

And do not be conformed to this world, but be transformed by the renewing of your mind, that you may prove what is that good and acceptable and perfect will of God.

Those who fail to embrace an uncomfortable transformation will become more conformed to the world around them.

The enemies of the Church are as hate-filled and vicious as any earthly terrorist. Satan, the world, and our flesh have been winning the war against God's people for the last seventy-five years. The chaos of the 2020s provides an opportunity for the final blow. Many have already surrendered and more will follow **without knowing it.**

> *The coming of the lawless one is according to the working of Satan, with all power, signs, and lying wonders, and with all unrighteous deception among those who perish, because they did not receive the love of the truth, that they might be saved. And for this reason God will send them strong delusion, that they should believe the lie (2 Thessalonians 2:9-11).*

Our enemies' primary weapon is deception. The power of deception lies in its nature: people who are deceived do not know that they are. The only solution is a love for the truth—a love that must be received. Failure to receive a love of the truth results in a God-imposed delusion.

The sidelines—where most Christians attempt to live out their faith—have become a kind of "no man's land". Failing to take a strong stand with God against Satan, the world, and our carnal mind, many Christians now find themselves at odds with both sides. Of course, this is not God's heart for His children. He longs for their spiritual safety and strength. With His Son and Spirit, He will deliver and transform all who will participate in their good work.

Our Desires and Mission

> *Delight yourself also in the Lord,*
> *And He shall give you the desires of your heart*
> *(Psalm 37:4).*

inLight Consulting was birthed out of a heart's desire to help Christian leaders find joyful, Spirit-filled ministry.

Surrendered to God, desires become missions, shared with God for the advancement of His kingdom. The mission of inLight Consulting is to encourage, edify, and equip leaders in the workplace to become disciple makers and transformation agents. A workplace leader is anyone with a sphere of influence in the workplace (including the religious workplace and the home).

God uses inLight Consulting to put courage into leaders, build them up in His word and will, and help them find healing and unity for the good works He has created for them to walk in (Ephesians 2:10). We accomplish this through one-on-one and group discipling, and through blogs and books. We desire to see Matthew 5:16 manifested through these leaders for our Father's glory; that they might experience the greater-than life Jesus promised to those who believe in Him (John 14:12). Furthermore, we are convinced that these leaders will become houses who stand in the storms of life, as beacons to those less prepared (Matthew 7:26-27).

Our Purpose in This Book

Our first book, *The Map Maker* (2014), encouraged Christian leaders to discover the desire of their heart for kingdom adventure and to bring others along with them in God's good work. This book introduces a new perspective and metaphor.

In the coming decade, houses will fall and the people and institutions those houses represent will be looking around for refuge, encouragement, and understanding. This will include individuals and corporate entities we know of as "Christian". The potential opportunities for positive kingdom impact are exceedingly, abundantly beyond what we can imagine. I truly believe this is God's answer to our prayers for revival—the brokenness of idols and the death-to-self required for transformation.

The Christian leaders—the real leaders—of the coming decade will be those individuals, families, and fellowships who have assessed the foundations of their houses, pursued the necessary deconstruction and restoration, and surrendered to God's sacrificial love for others. Our purpose in this book is to help Christians—those who are and will become leaders—navigate the chaos and storms of the 2020s in God's ways.

Our Thesis

God uses chaos to drive a wedge between our spirit man and the world. His call to come out of the world must be answered. Chaos forces us to come off the fence. Stepping down on the wrong side will lead to deeper conformity with the world; responding rightly will lead to transformation by the renewal of our minds (Romans 12:2). This applies to individuals, groups, and fellowships of all sizes.

God will allow the chaos to create a suffering to separate our spirit man and our flesh. As we argued in *An Enemy Lies Within* (2020), the carnal mind (i.e., the mind of our flesh) has been the #1 enemy of God's people since we rebelled against Him by eating from the Tree of the Knowledge of Good and Evil. Those willing to endure the suffering will come to know and loathe their whiny, blame-shifting, excuse-making flesh while turning to their Father in heaven for understanding, comfort, and strength. The key is to maximize the suffering for God's glory and our maturity.

Lastly, God is a process-oriented problem solver. The journey is as important as the end result. In fact, you cannot have the end result without the journey. The process God provides to separate our spirit man from the world and our flesh is transformation. We will apply this process using the metaphor of house inspection, renovation, and abiding.

This Study

Based on Jesus' closure to the Sermon on the Mount, we could simply encourage each other to hear and do the sayings found there. But what does that look like for a Twenty-first Century Christian who may have a shallow or faulty foundation? Becoming the Christian described in the Beatitudes is a lifetime pursuit. How can we be sure our houses are strong and secure right now?

While we certainly recommend in-depth and regular study of the Sermon on the Mount, we suggest the inspection and restoration process offered here prior to any further attempts at "adding-on". Stressing our strong conviction in this matter is hard to do without getting distractingly negative about the state of the church. To avoid that trap, please allow me to leave it at this: there is much for the average Christian to unlearn and much foundation building that has been ignored.

For those comfortable with the stability of their foundation and the security of their house, we have provided a short list of Jesus' sayings in the Appendix. Take a moment and test yourself. How many of our Lord's sayings are you doing? How many have you considered? How many could you have listed?

For those more concerned, please consider that every house renovation begins with an inspection, our obvious first step. Are we thinking rightly about God's kingdom and His purposes for the church? Have we been deceived, distracted, or lulled to sleep? How will we respond when the storms rage against our house? What will we do when weak spots are exposed?

God's purpose in the storms is the inspection, testing, and ultimate perfection of our houses. Except for the most mature Christian, inspection exposes shallowness, cracks, and weak construction. Repair and remediation must quickly follow inspection, lest the storms catch us unprepared. Ignorance is bliss only until the moment your house comes tumbling down.

It is important to recognize, God has both the grace and desire to fully restore our houses. He simply wants our cooperation. That is not to suggest navigating the chaos is easy. For many of us, it will be the hardest thing we have ever done, and the reason we need to walk with others.

Once the structural issues have been repaired to God's satisfaction, our final consideration will be His way for our abiding. With Christ abiding in us and us in Him, how do we respond to the storms of this decade and the destruction they produce. While the full breadth of the abiding life is beyond this study, we will touch on some of the responsibilities and opportunities entrusted to the inhabitants of strong houses. These include the refuge, encouragement, and building up of others (i.e., making disciples).

Making the Most of It

Books are written to be read, but reading this book will not make your house strong enough to stand in the chaos and storms of this decade. This book will not help you apart from relational prayer with God and should therefore function as a tool for your conversations with Him. Faith comes by hearing, and hearing by the *rhema* (i.e., spoken) word of God (Romans 10:17). Only the grace of God, appropriated by faith, can prepare and protect us.

To encourage and foster your relationship with the Father, Son, and Holy Spirit, we have included a lot of questions—particularly in the inspection section. Here are a few you should already be asking:

1. What does a strong house look like? How does my house compare? Is the foundation complete and well anchored?
2. What are God's ways for constructing and restoring houses? Do my ways align with His? Am I committed to finding and following His way?
3. What are God's purposes in the storms and for my house in the midst of them?

Many of the questions you encounter will be intentionally left unanswered. They are questions best answered by God, not man. Take time to listen; the most critical thing we will need in the storms is a recognition of God's voice. Some have learned God's voice in solitude; for me, the recognition of His voice came through times of corporate prayer. Both are important investments of time and attention.

Of course, the Holy Bible is an important resource for understanding God's purposes for the storms. We reference it extensively in this study. It will serve you well to keep yours close by.

Furthermore, faith you acquire will die without accompanying good works (James 2:20). After all, good works that glorify our Father in heaven are the reason we are saved in the first place (Ephesians 2:8-10; Matthew 5:16). The difference between a house who stands and falls is found in the doing or not doing of Matthew 7:24-27. It will be a waste of your time to store up the facts, truths, perspectives, and propositions found in this book for some potential later use. Please do not read this book to get to the end of it. If God speaks to you along the way, let His word encourage, edify, and equip you—then obey as the Holy Spirit leads.

Finally, let me suggest three additional considerations. First, God knows our frame and is dynamic and specific in His working in us to both will and to do for His good pleasure. It is important to trust His work in ourselves and in others. In the end, it will all make kingdom sense. Trust the Holy Spirit to guide you.

Secondly, this book has been written in response to the storms which have come to America and to the church that resides here. However, it will serve you well to recognize the truths presented here apply to every storm of life (e.g., cancer, loss of a loved one, persecution). These storms are allowed to test our faith, and to prove and prepare us for future tribulations. There is a time when the opportunity to prepare has passed. Start now; for the time is growing short.

Thirdly, I encourage you to read these articles from three perspectives. First, read them from the perspective of your own preparation. Only the prepared are positioned to help prepare others. Second, consider those in your spheres of influence, for you are responsible, and will benefit, from their preparation. Most importantly, consider God's perspective in your preparation. Focus on Him and His pleasure. Use the talents you have been given wisely. Behold the glory of the Lord, and you will be transformed into the very same image—a light and a refuge for the brethren (2 Corinthians 3:18, Matthew 5:16).

One Very Important Caveat

Some or many of you may notice, I am not a biblical scholar, nor a seminary graduate. My highest aim is to be a good pen. That is not a false humility. I truly find joy in being the real Author's writing instrument. With that in mind, please remember the truths you find in this book may not mean all that I believe they mean, but they must mean something. I trust the Father, Son, and Holy Spirit will help you put meaning to them for your response to the chaos and storms of this life, and the decade ahead.

CHAPTER 1

Why Storms and Chaos?

And we know that all things work together for good to those who love God, to those who are the called according to His purpose (Romans 8:28).

Storms and the chaos they produce come in many shapes and sizes. A thunderstorm recently blew through with winds strong enough to break a dying tree limb into our neighbor's house. The only things damaged were a small portion of the gutter and my wallet. In return, I got to know my new neighbors better. It certainly could have been worse.

Our trip to New Orleans after Hurricane Katrina left an mark on my psyche. On the trip down there, we drove through more than a hundred miles of pine trees broken off approximately forty feet from the ground, as far as the eye could see. That eerie scene turned out to be small preparation for what we would find in the Ninth Ward: Houses washed blocks away from their foundations, a school filled with four feet of mud, very little emergency power, and very few people. The house we worked to restore had to have sheetrock removed more than twelve feet from ground level. I cannot imagine what it must have been like in the midst of that storm.

Emotional, psychological, and spiritual storms also come in varying shapes and sizes. Some are hardly noticeable, while others threaten our sanity and challenge our faith. Only the youngest of us have been spared from the loss of loved ones, battles with debilitating injury and disease, or agonizing, dark nights of the soul.

People respond differently to similar storms. There were people who left New Orleans to never come back, while others stayed or quickly returned to rebuild. Similarly, one child will handle the loss of a parent better than another. Psychology, psychiatry, and counseling are demanding professions for a reason. Everyone could use a little help with their storms now and then. Of course, where one goes for help is key and something we will touch on in a moment.

As different as storms and people are, a common denominator exists between them: storms test, prove, and (most often) strengthen the people who come in contact with them. In fact, God creates and allows storms and the chaos they produce for this very purpose.

God trusts some of His people with bigger storms, knowing they will respond in a way that brings Him greater glory. I simply can't imagine myself doing very well spiritually in the persecution many Christians around the world are facing, though I am encouraged by the countless testimonies I have read and heard of the Holy Spirit rising up inside someone to give them strength for holy faithfulness.

What then are we to do about our problems? We must learn to live with them until such time as God delivers us from them. If we cannot remove them, then we must pray for grace to endure them without murmuring. Problems patiently endured will work for our spiritual perfecting. They harm us only when we resist them or endure them unwillingly. (Tozer, 2015)

The way we handle storms has much to do with the success we will have with them in the future. The Bible gives us much to think about in this regard.

The Opportunity for Deception

When natural storms come, the wicked prey on the helpless. Scams and price gouging are common themes in every disaster. The chaos gives opportunity for the strong to take advantage of the weak.

The storms and chaos they produce will give the same opportunity to our spiritual enemies. They will fight us tooth and nail to keep the knowledge of God hidden from His children and the world. The agents of deception are all around us.

> So the great dragon was cast out, that serpent of old, called the Devil and Satan, **who deceives the whole world**; he was cast to the earth, and his angels were cast out with him (Revelation 12:9).

> And Jesus answered and said to them: "Take heed that **no one deceives you**." (Matthew 24:4).

> If anyone among you thinks he is religious, and does not bridle his tongue but **deceives his own heart**, this one's religion is useless (James 1:26).

So, let's take an eyes-open and honest inventory of the deceptors in our lives: Satan, the world, and even our own minds are potential sources of deception. Of course, this is true in every minute of every hour of every day in a Christian's life. We don't always notice; for that is the nature of deception—it is... well, deceptive.

3

Storms tend to intensify the opportunity for deception; particularly if the storms we see approaching are a part of the end-of-days tribulations that will usher in the Day of the Lord, and "The Tribulation". Jesus and Paul warned of such things.

> *And because lawlessness will abound, the love of many will grow cold. But he who endures to the end shall be saved (Matthew 24:12-13).*

> *Let no one deceive you by any means; for that Day will not come unless the falling away comes first, and the man of sin is revealed, the son of perdition... according to the working of Satan, with all power, signs, and lying wonders, and with all unrighteous deception among those who perish, because they did not receive the love of the truth, that they might be saved. And for this reason God will send them strong delusion, that they should believe the lie, that they all may be condemned who did not believe the truth but had pleasure in unrighteousness (2 Thessalonians 2:3, 9-12).*

Two things of note: First, both Jesus and Paul warn that many will be deceived. It will help your understanding to stop and consider what "many" means. Is it six out of ten? Eight out of ten? Whatever you decide, I bet its more than you thought possible.

Second, don't be deceived to think the deception is reserved for those outside of your church fellowship. In fact, careful reading will reveal the deception spoken of in each of these passages is the deception of church "members". For example, the falling away in 2 Thessalonians is a falling away from the faith (you have to be in something to fall away from it). So, please don't be naïve about the deceptions that have already come upon the church; and will intensify in the soon-coming days.

Now, with all this in mind, it is important to note that storms are not all bad. They offer great opportunity for God to show Himself strong and faithful. Furthermore, He often uses the storms in our lives to reveal the deceptions that have come against us. Of course, it is better to discover and deal with the deception before the storms hit, for then we are positioned to be a refuge and guide for others—an instrument for their salvation, sanctification and transformation.

Four Biblical Perspectives

The perspectives we take with us into the storms of life are critical, make-or-break paradigms. If we think like the world, we will seek worldly solutions. This is the only option for most of mankind. Christians, on the other hand, have the perspective of heaven (Ephesians 2:6). We would be foolish to set our minds on anything else. We therefore offer the following perspectives for your edification and encouragement. We will cover each of these more fully in subsequent chapters.

Chaos and Caterpillars

But we all, with unveiled face, beholding as in a mirror the glory of the Lord, are being transformed into the same image from glory to glory, just as by the Spirit of the Lord (2 Corinthians 3:18).

Consider the ugly, leaf-bound, leaf-eating caterpillar who *metamorphoos* into a beautiful, free-flying, nectar-eating butterfly (the Greek for transformed is *metamorphoo*). Trusting in the process, the caterpillar dies to his old ways and form, to become a glorious new form of God's creation.

5

Similarly, God will use the chaos of this decade to dramatically transform the individuals, families, and fellowships who keep their eyes focused on the Lord and their minds set on things above. The Holy Spirit waits for God's people to submit to His transforming—*metamorphooing*—work.

Our response to this work will require leaving something behind. Many times, it is security, long-held beliefs, routines, even people and places we have grown to love. Rarely does this call not involve a dying to ourselves. And so, there must be grieving—something best done with others.

It will help us (and those we love) to remember that chaos is normal for every Christian committed to following Jesus Christ. Sacrifice marked the life of Jesus, and He sent us as the Father sent Him (John 20:21). As He did with His Son, our Father in heaven has great purpose for the chaos He introduces or allows in our life.

What person in Christ do you desire to be? What does becoming a butterfly look like with you?

Storms and Houses

> *Therefore whoever hears these sayings of Mine, and does them, I will liken him to a wise man who built his house on the rock: and the rain descended, the floods came, and the winds blew and beat on that house; and it did not fall, for it was founded on the rock.*
>
> *But everyone who hears these sayings of Mine, and does not do them, will be like a foolish man who built his house on the sand: and the rain descended, the floods came, and the winds blew and beat on that house; and it fell. And great was its fall (Matthew 7:24-27).*

The storms we face in the coming decade will destroy the houses of people around us, exposing illegitimate or poorly founded relationships with God. It will be good for them to discover the insecure state of their salvation. Furthermore, they will be less likely to turn from God if they can find a strong house of refuge nearby. Becoming that house will include our own testing and humble response.

Unfortunately, many of us are quite good at avoiding storms and chaos. It seems like the sensible thing to do, right? The answer is a resounding "yes", unless God has intended them for our good.

Do we believe God works all things to the good of those who love Him and are called to His purpose (Romans 8:28)? If the answer is, "We'll see", then we do not believe it. The storms and chaos are not intended to prove Him, but us!

The storms of life measure our obedience and love for our King. Whether we like to admit it or not, such tests are for our good: to expose weak foundations and shoddily built structures.

As a side note: "Glass half empty" people must force them-selves to look optimistically into the storms. It will help to recognize: the chaos may serve as an answer to our prayers for a lost or wandering soul; and our strong house as God's intended refuge on the way to their salvation.

When was the last time you asked for a thorough inspection of your proverbial house?

Who will likely be looking to you for refuge, encourage-ment, and understanding?

Crossroads and Gates

And do not be conformed to this world, but be trans-formed by the renewing of your mind, that you may prove what is that good and acceptable and perfect will of God (Romans 12:2).

Then one said to Him, "Lord, are there few who are saved?" And He said to them, "Strive to enter through the narrow gate, for many, I say to you, will seek to enter and will not be able." (Luke 13:24).

As we know, God provides two ways from which all of mankind must choose. These are the broad way leading to destruction and the difficult way leading to eternal life (Matthew 7:13-14). Jesus tells us that between the two there is a narrow gate His followers, coming off the broad road, must strive to enter.

In my mind's eye, I picture a large group of church attenders loitering around outside the gate, waiting for someone to usher them into the kingdom. Many will even seek to enter and will not be able. Why? Because they did not know or were unwilling to strive.

This begs the question: What does Jesus mean by striving? Of course, striving is not about working for our salvation. We are saved by grace, through faith. So, what is the point of striving in this perspective?

For the sake of brevity, let me cut to the chase. Entering a narrow gate requires leaving baggage behind—laying aside every weight and sin that so easily ensnares us (Hebrews 12:1). It also requires discipline to hear and recognize God's voice, that we might find encouragement and direction. Eventually, entering through the narrow gate will require our striving to make a difficult and eternally significant decision.

This is an unpopular Christian perspective because it involves strenuous action, and it forces a decision. Romans 12:2 describes a crossroad: a point of decision between conformity with the world and our transformation into kingdom citizens.

Like those loitering outside the narrow gate, and those adept at avoiding storms and chaos, many of us have been standing at the crossroad of Romans 12:2 trying to find an easier way which is still acceptable to God. The storms of the 2020s will expose this thinking as compromise and deception. God will force us beyond the crossroad.

What do you make of Jesus' encouragement to strive?

Are you prepared to make some hard decisions?

Sidelines and Battlefields

You therefore must endure hardship as a good soldier of Jesus Christ. No one engaged in warfare entangles himself with the affairs of this life, that he may please him who enlisted him as a soldier (2 Timothy 2:3-4).

Therefore take up the whole armor of God, that you may be able to withstand in the evil day, and having done all, to stand (Ephesians 6:13).

For if anyone is a hearer of the word and not a doer, he is like a man observing his natural face in a mirror; for he observes himself, goes away, and immediately forgets what kind of man he was (James 1:23-24).

There are a couple of reasons why most Christians would rather sit on the sidelines than get in the game. First of all, what is going on around us is not a game at all. It is a war, and who in their carnal minds wants to get involved in that? You know, I think our subconscious gravitation toward the sideline explains why spectator sports are so popular. Living vicariously through others is both entertaining and safe.

Secondly, putting on the whole armor of God every day is a distraction from the entertainment of this world. It takes time to take up salvation, faith, righteousness, truth, and the word of God. Wearing the armor makes us look weird to our neighbors. Being a good soldier requires a level of disentanglement with the affairs of this life that is both uncomfortable and sacrificial.

Of course, sitting on the sidelines—whether in a pew, stadium seat, or comfortable chair in front of the TV—means we are hearers of the word and not doers. Sadly, many Christians have forgotten the kind of men and women we are created to become. So, let me be (perhaps) the first to tell you: You are a soldier, a warrior, a mighty man or woman of God! The only place for you right now, in the storms and chaos, is on the battlefield.

Are you properly dressed for the war?

Where do you see yourself on the battlefield (e.g., front lines, support, communications)?

Conclusion

> *Finally, my brethren, be strong in the Lord and in the power of His might (Ephesians 6:10).*

God carefully orchestrates time and space for His purposes. You and I—and those in our spheres of influence—are alive right now to become willing participants in the "exceedingly abundantly above all that we ask or think, according to the power that works in us" (Ephesians 3:20). So, let me remind and encourage you:

1. Caterpillars who refuse transformation will die as caterpillars.
2. Houses will either stand or fall.
3. The crossroad demands a decision, and entering requires striving.
4. Battles are not games, and they do not have sidelines.

The storms and chaos are intended to help us stop and consider these matters from a heavenly perspective.

Finally, remember God has grace for everything He desires and requires of us. The Father is working in us to will and to do for His good pleasure (Philippians 2:13), Jesus has promised to make us His followers (Mark 1:17), and the Holy Spirit is our helper, teacher, and transformer (John 14:16, 26; 2 Corinthians 3:18).

Yes, there will be sacrifice, tribulation, and even persecution; these are promised to all who follow Jesus (John 16:33). We can avoid wasting the pain by simply letting the Father, Son, and Holy Spirit have their way with us.

Remember, the light at the end of the tunnel is the glory of God and His kingdom on earth!

Step One – Inspect

CHAPTER 2

Better to Get Your House Inspected Now

Those who live in the path of regular and catastrophic storm activity (e.g., the American Gulf Coast and the Midwest) have a heightened appreciation for the preparation required to survive such eventualities. They want to know their roof will not go flying off in the high winds and turbulence. They want to know their house will not float away in the flood—to know that it has been securely anchored to a firm foundation. They want to be reasonably confident the walls and ceilings of their house will hold up under the storm's pressure; and their whole house is water tight.

In anticipation of the coming storm, I have decided to request a heart inspection. I don't want to be surprised by a weakness in my relationship with the Lord, a fault in my character, or a lack of faith in His keeping power. I want an increased assurance I will trust Him and keep my eyes on Him, even in the most violent storm. More than anything, I want to know I will remain steadfast in my commitment to His purposes and ways in my life.

I want the same for you. So, I hope you will join me in my request for an inspection. The process begins with a simple prayer:

Search me, O God, and know my heart;
Try me, and know my anxieties;
And see if there is any wicked way in me,
And lead me in the way everlasting (Psalm 139:23-24).

For your encouragement, here are two examples of His faithful work in me:

1. **Trust:** The most obvious and influential characteristic in the life of the man whose house will withstand a storm is his trust in the Lord. Consequently, God has been sending tests and trials my way—to "try me, and know my anxieties". He is teaching me not only to trust Him but how to find trust in the midst of a storm. For the most part, it has simply been learning to recognize and intentionally confess I trust Him with whatever the test or trial may be. I do this every morning, and throughout the day; sometimes silently and sometimes out loud. He has also encouraged me to tell others I am learning to trust Him in these areas (my confession to the brethren).

2. **Pride:** The Lord has rooted pride out of me on several significant (and painful) occasions. While I once thought, "that must be the last of it", I am now not so naïve to think all my pride is gone. Sure enough, the Lord has exposed some more of "this wicked way in me". In this case, it is the pride that expects to be treated in an acceptable, non-offensive way; a pride that turns inward toward self-pity and self-defense. This type of pride will be an especially dangerous enemy in a storm which includes persecution and suffering for the kingdom of God. I have been leveraging 1 John 1:9—*If we confess our sins, He is faithful*

and just to forgive us our sins and to cleanse us from all unrighteousness—in dealings with the pride in my life.

God desires to lead each one of His children "in the way everlasting". He loves us so much, He will allow storms in our lives to search and try us. He will spare no pain to make us free and prepare us for the marriage supper of the Lamb. In His mercy, He is willing to inspect our houses before a big storm comes. I hope these examples have encouraged you to invite inspection. The time is growing short!

Before we move on, let me clarify something: The storms we are experiencing are not "The Storm", meaning the Great Tribulation. As we see in Matthew 24 and Mark 13, Jesus taught there would be small "t" tribulations before the big "T" occurs. This should be sobering news, particularly for those who think they are going to avoid tribulation and suffering via a pre-Tribulation escape plan.

Spiritual Preparation is Paramount

And now a word for the preppers (of which I am one). Prepping physically (e.g., storing food and ensuring a sustainable water source) is not a sign of weak faith, but of wisdom. However, preparing spiritually must become the paramount objective for everyone who believes a storm is coming. This is contrary to our protective nature; and contrary to what most of the world is promoting.

Even in the church, many are encouraging—and selling— physical preparations (e.g., freeze dried food, hedge funds, guns and ammo, leaving the country). When you look at it from their perspective, you quickly learn there are hundreds of things each of us could do in the natural realm to protect ourselves and our families from the storm.

And that is the problem!

How do we know which things to do? Do we use our rational mind to figure out strategy and plan? The number of contingencies would make any such plan impossible to execute. There are simply too many variables. So, do we do everything necessary to cover every possibility? Most of us lack the time and finances for that approach.

Our only hope for doing the right things is to position ourselves to hear, understand, and obey the voice of God. This is not new to our walk with the Lord; but the stakes have grown considerably. Hopefully, the urgency we feel in the physical will motivate us to find the center of God's will in our preparations.

With this in mind, let me encourage you: finding the center of God's will is possible for every one of His children. All we must do is surrender ourselves to His purposes. The greatest of those are no different than they have been since mankind's rebellion. In the end, we will enjoy the restoration of all He has lost.

> *And I heard a loud voice from the throne saying, "Look! God's dwelling place is now among the people, and he will dwell with them. They will be his people, and God himself will be with them and be their God." (Revelation 21:3).*

At the end of the story (as we know it right now), God will get back three things He lost in the beginning:

1. *"He will dwell with them"*—It was always God's intention to inhabit His people. Jesus spoke of its beginning in John 14:23: *"If anyone loves Me, he will keep*

My word; and My Father will love him, and We will come to him and make Our home with him." This spiritual reality will be physically manifested in the New Jerusalem.

God will restore the habitation He intended to have with His people.

2. *"They shall be His people"*—We can only imagine the depths of intimacy God had with Adam and Eve in the Garden—and His loss in their rebellion. God sent Jesus to make a way for the restoration of His relationship with us. Jesus prayed the will of the Father back to Him in John 17:

> *And this is eternal life, that they may know You, the only true God, and Jesus Christ whom You have sent (verse 3).*

> *… that they all may be one, as You, Father, are in Me, and I in You; that they also may be one in Us (verse 21).*

God will fully restore the intimate relationship He intended to have with His children.

3. *"God Himself will be… their God"*—The third thing God lost in the Garden was His reign in the hearts of His people. Before they disobeyed God's command regarding the Tree of the Knowledge of Good and Evil, Adam and Eve determined they were better suited to make decisions for themselves. They determined to be their own kings. They rebelled against God in a futile attempt to become like Him.

God will fully restore His reign in the hearts of His subjects.

If we will passionately and urgently pursue these purposes, we will find the center of His will for every season of our lives; including the coming season of storm and chaos. Our preparation must begin here; and it must begin now. Time is running out!

Our King is a good king. He desires to say, "Well done, good and faithful servant." I believe He has made Himself available—right now—to help us assess our level of preparedness. I believe He is looking to show Himself strong on behalf of those who are loyal to Him and His Father. I believe it will be a good thing to receive His gracious correction and His wise counsel regarding our preparation for the coming storm.

CHAPTER 3

God's Eternal Purposes—
A Framework for Inspection

*And we know that all things work together for good to
those who love God, to those who are the called according
to His purpose. For whom He foreknew, He also predes-
tined to be conformed to the image of His Son, that He
might be the firstborn among many brethren. Romans
8:28-29*

Many in the body of Christ recognize the inevitability
of ongoing societal, political, economic, and spiritual
storms and have consequently become concerned about the
impact these will have on the church. The shutting-in and
shutting-down of 2020 has provided a season for reflec-
tion over the state of the church and our personal spiritual
condition. The desire for more of God has replaced laissez
faire attitudes with a growing urgency for preparation. We
hope many more will come to realize God's purpose in our
preparation extends beyond personal and physical protection
to the opportunities chaos presents for the advancement of
His kingdom.

With storms here and on the way, it is more important than
ever to find the center of God's will and the good work He
has created for us to walk in (Ephesians 2:10). His will and
way turn chaos into adventure, replace fear with faith, and

strengthen our houses to stand as refuge for others. This is the normal Christian life; so how do we find it?

Our pursuit of God's eternal purposes—His reign over our hearts, His intimacy with us, and His habitation in us—will supernaturally propel us into His will for this strategic season. There is a biblical way to assess our preparedness and receive wisdom and revelation in the ways God would have us strengthen our house. In fact, we are encouraged and commanded to do exactly that:

> *Let us search out and examine our ways,*
> *And turn back to the Lord;*
> *Let us lift our hearts and hands*
> *To God in heaven (Lamentations 3:40-41).*

> *For I say, through the grace given to me, to everyone who is among you, not to think of himself more highly than he ought to think, but to think soberly, as God has dealt to each one a measure of faith (Romans 12:3).*

> *Examine yourselves as to whether you are in the faith. Test yourselves. Do you not know yourselves, that Jesus Christ is in you?—unless indeed you are disqualified (2 Corinthians 13:5).*

These passages are clear on a few points: First, we are encouraged to seek God's inspection; second, we are commanded to inspect ourselves (both personally and in community); and third, this inspection is for our good and for the good of God's kingdom.

Inspecting Our House for His Reign

Many in the church have grown up with the philosophies of a "democratic republic". Democracy has been a great political experiment. However, it has created a cultural mindset which makes it difficult to live in a healthy relationship with God. In God's kingdom, there is no "of the people, by the people, for the people".

> *For of Him and through Him and to Him are all things, to whom be glory forever. Amen (Romans 11:36).*

All things in the kingdom of God are of, through, and to Him. He is the one who determines and executes mercy and justice. Our rights are what He determines them to be. He has the only and final vote.

For the rebellious, this is an unacceptable situation. And that is exactly what got us into this mess. The first sin was more than disobedience; it was outright rebellion. Before Adam and Eve disobeyed God, they decided they should determine what was best for themselves. They decided they would become the captains of their ship. They mutinied, and all was lost (for a time).

Thankfully, God has a plan to take back the throne of mankind's heart. Reestablishing His reign is one of God's greatest pursuits. Restoring His reign on the throne of our hearts will come easier once we understand the gospel of the kingdom, its place in God's story, and our place in His kingdom.

Now after John was put in prison, Jesus came to Galilee, preaching the gospel of the kingdom of God, and saying, "The time is fulfilled, and the kingdom of God is at hand. Repent, and believe in the gospel." (Mark 1:14-15).

What gospel are we to believe? The gospel of the kingdom is the full gospel. It is more than the good news of Jesus Christ's death, burial, and resurrection. Though it is of first importance, the good news most have been taught is only a part of the gospel of the kingdom, for the gospel of the kingdom is literally "the good news of God's reign in the hearts of His children".

Consequently, when Jesus preached "repent", He meant we were to turn from self-rule to His kingdom rule. We are commanded to move from rebellion to surrender. Our surrender must be humble and absolute; the Creator will not share His reign with the created. In our surrendered state, we are positioned to receive all God has purposed for our lives.

The gospel of the kingdom was the major theme of Jesus' preaching in all of Galilee and throughout Israel.

And Jesus went about all Galilee, teaching in their synagogues, preaching the gospel of the kingdom, and healing all kinds of sickness and all kinds of disease among the people. (Matthew 4:23).

Now when it was day, He departed and went into a deserted place. And the crowd sought Him and came to Him, and tried to keep Him from leaving them; but He said to them, "I must preach the kingdom of God to the other cities also, because for this purpose I have been sent." (Luke 4:42-43).

Jesus was sent with a purpose: To preach the gospel of the kingdom everywhere He went. It was not just for private conversations with His disciples. It was good news for everyone. As you might expect, the gospel of the kingdom continued to be preached after Jesus ascended to sit at His Father's right hand.

> *But when they believed Philip as he preached the things concerning the kingdom of God and the name of Jesus Christ, both men and women were baptized (Acts 8:12).*

> *So when they had appointed him [Paul] a day, many came to him at his lodging, to whom he explained and solemnly testified of the kingdom of God, persuading them concerning Jesus from both the Law of Moses and the Prophets, from morning till evening (Acts 28:23).*

For more references on the gospel of the kingdom, see Matthew 9:35; 10:7; 24:14; Luke 8:1; 9:2, 6, 11; 10:9; Acts 1:3; 8:12; 19:8; 20:25.

Jesus—our good King—came to inaugurate and establish the kingdom of His Father. As a good king, He made clear the requirements of our entry into that kingdom. In preparation for our inspection, we will look at His expectations from two perspectives, beginning with the Parable of the Talents. Please read Matthew 25:14-30 and consider the following:

1. "Talents" are more than money. They are every good thing God has given us for life and godliness (2 Peter 1:3).
2. This parable does not include a servant who buried half of the talent given to him. Our obedience is an all-or-nothing condition with Jesus.

3. Misunderstanding and self-deception are not accept-able excuses.
4. The difference between reward and consequence is vast.

Jesus explained the requirements of entry into His Father's kingdom in this and other parables. The parables of the Wise and Foolish Virgins (Matthew 25:1-13) and the Wedding Feast (Matthew 22:1-14) come to mind. He spoke more directly about counting the cost of being His disciple in Luke 14:25-33, where He describes in stark detail a few of His conditions:

1. Our love for Jesus must make every other love a distant second. To make the point, He uses a very strong word to describe (in hyperbole) just how distant the second loves must be. Jesus is jealous for His Bride.
2. For each of us, to become a disciple of Christ requires our following Him in an absolutely sacrificial walk; including the complete denial of self (Luke 9:23) and the forsaking of all we have.
3. By the grace He supplies, we must refuse—even refuse to desire (Luke 9:24)—our inalienable rights as humans. We must make ourselves "of no reputation, taking the form of a bondservant" (Philippians 2:5-7).

These are but a few of the many requirements Jesus has graciously and pragmatically laid out for the inspection of our condition in this area of His reign. We will cover a few others in the inspection scorecard, at the end of this chapter.

Inspecting Our House for Intimacy

And this is eternal life, that they may know You, the only true God, and Jesus Christ whom You have sent (John 17:3).

It is impossible to love someone you do not know. And so, it is no coincidence our primary desire toward God—eternal life—is to know Him and His Son in the most intimate way possible. The Greek word translated "know" in this verse describes the deepest relationship between two people.

Know (*ginōskō*): Learn to know, come to know, get a knowledge of, perceive, feel; to become known; Jewish idiom for sexual intercourse between a man and a woman (*Outline of Biblical Usage, BlueLetterBible.org*).

This is much different from the knowing associated with intellectual and moral understanding (*gnōsis*).

The normal Christian life is a life of growing in relational knowledge of God. How awesome to know from the start that the One who has identified Himself as the truth encourages us to an intimate relationship with Himself, and with our Father in heaven!

As we begin this inspection, let us commit ourselves to be motivated, sustained, and completed by the chief desire of God's heart for us: that we would love Him with all our heart, with all our soul, with all our mind, and with all our strength (Mark 12:30). Let us commit ourselves to fight for what has been given to us: to know God, that we might love Him more.

There has never been a more critical time for the followers of Christ to search out this matter of intimacy with their Maker.

> *Call my people to repentance. Yea, call them to their knees for prayer and fasting, for confession and vigilance. For this is a strategic hour. The enemy is rejoicing already over his anticipated victories. Ye can disappoint him and thwart his evil designs if ye lay hold upon the throne of God in steadfast, believing prayer.*
> (Roberts, 1973)

This is a strategic hour—perhaps the most strategic hour in the history of the church. Something must be done. But what? "Only God knows" may have jumped into your mind. So, why don't we ask Him? That is exactly what He desires for us.

Every Christian knows the effective fervent prayer of a righteous man avails much (James 5:16). Prayer is powerful (at least it's supposed to be), and nothing of heavenly value is possible without prayer. So why do we struggle to pray, both individually and corporately? Why are we so unsure about the effectiveness of our prayers? Why does it seem so many of our prayers go unanswered? Why is our prayer life so ineffective, difficult, and dissatisfying?

We have lost God's way and purpose in prayer because our enemies have become very effective in cutting off our communication with God! It is time we fought back!

The first strategic move in every war is to cut off communications between the forces on the ground and the central command center. Consequently, much energy and intelligence is focused on keeping the lines of communication open. The situation is no different in the war we are fighting against Satan. We must be fiercely diligent to defend what we have been given: The means for effective communication—and relationship—with God.

Prayer (*deēsis*): Need, indigence, want, privation, extreme poverty; a seeking, asking, entreating, entreaty to God or to man. From *deomai*: to want, lack; to desire, long for; to ask, beg; the thing asked for; to pray, make supplications (*Outline of Biblical Usage, BlueLetterBible.org*).

There are three things to notice about the definition of prayer. First, it is more about need than want. Second, that need comes from an extreme sense of poverty (i.e., it is humble). Third, prayer includes seeking and desiring—its relational aspects.

It is no coincidence God has made prayer man's most powerful weapon in the battle for the kingdom. God is most intimate in revealing His plans and encouraging His children in this place. As we battle with Him through prayer, He establishes His relationship with us. There is no more important thing we can do in our preparation for the coming storms and chaos.

Inspecting Our House for His Habitation

It is impossible to assess the foundation and structure of our house without first knowing the vision God has for it. He has, in His wisdom, provided that vision for us in Paul's letter to the Church at Ephesus.

> *And He Himself gave some to be apostles, some prophets, some evangelists, and some pastors and teachers, for the equipping of the saints for the work of ministry, for the edifying of the body of Christ, till we all come to the unity of the faith and of the knowledge of the Son of God, to a perfect man, to the measure of the stature of the fullness of Christ; that we should no longer be children, tossed to and fro and carried about with every wind of doctrine, by*

the trickery of men, in the cunning craftiness of deceitful plotting, but, speaking the truth in love, may grow up in all things into Him who is the head—Christ—from whom the whole body, joined and knit together by what every joint supplies, according to the effective working by which every part does its share, causes growth of the body for the edifying of itself in love. Ephesians 4:11-16

This is the church Christ envisioned—the church that would be His Bride. We are to be that church, for the LORD's habitation. This is our destiny. Every follower of Jesus Christ has a desire in their heart for the church described in this passage:

- Equipped *(katartismos):* to be fixed and fitted for its intended use (like a broken bone or a torn net).
- Unified in both the faith and the knowledge of the Son of God (not a collective compromise of human doctrines).
- No longer deceived (that's a big one for today).
- Able to speak the truth in love.
- Maturing in **all** things (i.e., transformed by the renewing of our minds).
- Knit tightly together (like a hug instead of a handshake, or a beautiful tapestry).
- Effectively working (the Greek here is *energeo*: the energy for ministry).
- Every part doing its share.
- A fellowship building itself up in sacrificial love (i.e., the Bride making herself ready).

Are you having the same thought I'm having? How is this possible? We are so far from this; it is difficult to even imagine such a thing. But God *"is able to do exceedingly abundantly above all that we ask or think, according to the power that works in us"* (Ephesians 3:20); and Jesus Christ will have His Bride.

Praise God, this unity is not up to us. In fact, things are moving along in spite of our failed efforts. Even in this day of apparent decline, we can be encouraged He has not been caught by surprise.

Yes, Jesus Christ is building His church (Matthew 16:18). Our responsibility is to walk in the good work His Father has prepared for our participation. Our responsibility—particularly those of us in positions of leadership—is to find the center of His will and remain there. To do anything else will lead us and others to tragic destruction.

> *"Not everyone who says to Me, 'Lord, Lord,' shall enter the kingdom of heaven, but he who does the will of My Father in heaven. Many will say to Me in that day, 'Lord, Lord, have we not prophesied in Your name, cast out demons in Your name, and done many wonders in Your name?' And then I will declare to them, 'I never knew you; depart from Me, you who practice lawlessness!'" Matthew 7:21-23*

To avoid the same tragic surprise these men encountered, we must inspect our houses in light of God's will, and what better place to find His will than in His eternal purposes? It is never too early, nor too late, to inspect our commitment to His reign, His desire for intimacy, and the community His Son is building. The stability of our foundation and the security of our house depend on it.

Inspection Scorecard

During my time in the corporate world, I received a performance review at least one time each year. Invariably, my review was precluded and supplemented by a self-assessment. Every once in a while, it included a peer review. This process was a great tool for both my development and the company's success.

It has occurred to me that my reviews were not only about my performance—a view into the past. They were also about opportunity: for me, the opportunity for monetary reward, advancement, continuing education, etc.; for the company, the opportunity to advance their vision, purposes, and plans.

Similarly, our good King wants the best for us. He wants us to prosper in His Father's kingdom. His requirements are more about opportunity than correction (read that again). As we examine ourselves, it is important to keep this notion of opportunity in the forefront of our minds.

So, consider for a moment that you are one of a company of believers, all attempting to follow the Boss—our Lord, Jesus Christ—as He works diligently to bring all things under His reign. How would you know you are making progress in your alignment with His purpose and objectives? How would you assess your progress?

Recognizing our motivation for improvement is for the pleasure of our Lord, consider the following statements. Don't spend a lot of time on each one. Instead, spend the bulk of your time in preparatory prayer—inviting God to examine your heart (Psalm 139:23-24). If a statement does not make sense in your context, go on to the next one. Rate each statement on a scale of zero to five, with zero being no evidence of attainment and five being a level you believe is pleasing to the Lord.

Surrender to God's Reign

How complete is your surrender to the reign of Jesus Christ?

1. Putting your love for Jesus Christ far above your love for others.
2. Following in Jesus' sacrificial footsteps.
3. Saying goodbye to all you have.
4. Denying yourself; losing your life for His sake.
5. Investing the resources God has entrusted to you into His kingdom.
6. Abiding in His word.
7. Loving the brethren as Jesus loves them (i.e., laying down your life).

Intimacy with God

How strong is your prayer life relative to each of the following categories?

1. Disciplined (time and energy set aside for developing relationship with God)
2. Relational (getting to know God rather than getting things from Him)
3. Fervent (urgent, passionate, with great need)
4. Expectant (full of faith in God's purposes, plans, and power)
5. Effectual (evidence of changes in the world around you)
6. Obedient (taking every thought captive)
7. Persistent (practicing His presence throughout the day)

With God in Community

How invested are you in community with God's people?

For Leaders:

1. Effectiveness in equipping the saints (i.e., preparing and repairing them for their intended use).
   a. Knowledge of their calling and ministry work.
   b. Awareness of their joy and satisfaction in ministry.
   c. Knowledge of their effectiveness and fruitfulness in ministry.
2. Unity of those in your spheres of influence.
   a. Demonstrations of their growing together in unity of the faith.
   b. Demonstrations of their growing together in knowledge of the Son of God.

For all the Saints (Leaders included):

1. Seeking to be equipped by your leaders.
2. Passionate engagement in your ministry work.
3. Ability to speak the truth in love.
4. Spiritual maturity of your personal walk with the Lord.
5. Intimacy with others in your fellowship.
6. Engagement in the day-to-day life of your fellowship.
7. Level of growth you have experienced in your fellowship in the last twelve months.

As you can see, there is much we can discover about ourselves through a healthy Spirit-led assessment. Our pursuit of a relationship with God in prayer is critical for the days ahead. The Spirit may bring other areas of opportunity to your mind. Give them your attention.

Lastly, do not be discouraged; that is not God's intention in this inspection. The vast majority of Christians find surrender, intimacy, and community extremely difficult. We have become distracted and deceived about what is important, but God will use the storms and chaos to get our attention and draw us back to Him. His ways are not difficult once we commit to them (Psalm 37:5-6).

Conclusion

So then each of us shall give account of himself to God (Romans 14:12).

After a long time the lord of those servants came and settled accounts with them (Matthew 25:19).

The Parable of the Talents is a most sobering passage (Matthew 25:14-30). From it, we discover there will come a day when we must give an account of what we have done with the "talents" of our stewardship. We do not know when that day will come, but we do know when it comes the time of preparation will be over. By God's grace, we know these things are true; and they are for our good.

Furthermore, we are learning the will and way of God, found in His eternal purposes, provides the foundation for our house inspection. Consideration of His purposes require the renewing of our minds, a primary work of the Holy Spirit. As we begin to think differently about our relationship with our heavenly Father, His Son, and the Holy Spirit, we will notice an unsuspecting enemy raising its ugly head. We will further expose that enemy and inspect the damage it has wrought in the next chapter.

CHAPTER 4

Renewed Thinking
for the Days Ahead[1]

*And do not be conformed to this world, but be trans-
formed by the renewing of your mind, that you may prove
what is that good and acceptable and perfect will of God.
Romans 12:2*

One of the problems with the way we think (a.k.a., mindset,
paradigm, worldview) is our thinking's subconscious
insistence that it is correct. Think about it (if your mind will
let you). What is the natural default assumption regarding
the way you think? It is so obvious, when you think about
it: Our minds assume they are thinking correctly. There is
one problem with that kind of thinking: it runs counter to
Romans 12:2.

Why would our minds need to be renewed if there was not
something wrong with them?

Our unwillingness to humbly recognize and confess we need
transformation inhibits the renewing of our minds. Having
the mind of Christ includes the humility to be suspicious
about the way we think—recognizing something is fundamentally wrong.

---

[1] Much of this chapter is excerpted from *An Enemy Lies Within* (Streetman,
2020).

Now get this: Doing so requires intentional and diligent effort. You might say there is a battle raging for the way we think—both individually and corporately.

Recognizing our need opens the door for the Holy Spirit to step in as our transformer. Only then will we "prove what is that good and acceptable and perfect will of God". This gives us hope for the church in America. This is one of the more significant reasons why the storms have come: to challenge the way we think, and to prove what we believe in our hearts.

God bless you with the grace to think humbly and the courage to pledge your full allegiance to the kingdom of God.

The Birth of An Enemy

For those who live according to the flesh set their minds on the things of the flesh, but those who live according to the Spirit, the things of the Spirit. For to be carnally minded is death, but to be spiritually minded is life and peace. Because the carnal mind is enmity against God; for it is not subject to the law of God, nor indeed can be (Romans 8:5-7).

In the greatest of ironic tragedies, Adam and Eve, eating from the Tree of the Knowledge of Good and Evil so they could be like God, not only condemned their lineage to spiritual death, but birthed in us an enemy of God. Their infamous decision forever linked the mind of carnal man to his rebellion. The carnal mind is enmity against God because it is rebellious, and cannot be anything else.

Mankind was not created to live from the Tree of the Knowledge of Good and Evil—attempting to survive and thrive from human reasoning about the right and wrong of things (Genesis 2:17). Those determinations belong to God. The kingdom of God is not a democracy; He decides what is good and evil. His people take Him at His word and obey accordingly.

Mankind was created by God to live by another tree, the Tree of Life, who is Christ.

> *Jesus said to him, "I am the way, the truth, and the life. No one comes to the Father except through Me." (John 14:6).*

> *For if when we were enemies we were reconciled to God through the death of His Son, much more, having been reconciled, we shall be saved by His life. (Romans 5:10).*

One might ask, "Why would the omniscient and omnipotent God create the Tree of the Knowledge of Good and Evil?" Two answers come to mind. First, the knowledge of good and evil is important and not the issue. It is attempting to live by that knowledge which makes us an enemy with our Creator.

Second, our choosing is important to God and remains so under the New Covenant. At our rebirth, we are given a new heart and spirit, but not a new mind (Ezekiel 36:22-27). We choose to follow the will of God or the mind of our carnal nature. Loving the LORD with all our mind is important to Him.

God desires a people who will choose Him every moment of every day. It is one of the amazing things about God, that after our failure in the Garden, He would continue to give us the choice of submitting to His reign, or continuing to live in rebellion to the One Who is love. Choosing His reign and love requires and empowers a continual overcoming of our carnal mind. In this regard, the carnal mind not only stands opposed to God, it works to inhibit our coming to God for deliverance from our rebellious, reasoning nature.

The Real #1

"The devil made me do it," popularized by Flip Wilson in the 1970s, has found its way into the Western church. It is the way we like to think. The devil is our most popular enemy. In our desire to shift blame, we have ignored one of the most astounding claims in all of Scripture:

> *Therefore submit to God. Resist the devil and he will flee from you (James 4:7).*

The devil has no power over the resisting Christian! It is really quite silly to blame him for our carnality.

The world has become another popular target for our blame-shifting and finger-pointing. Our government is a particularly favorite scapegoat. I experienced this several years ago while discussing the decline of Christian values in society with a brother in the Lord. Expressing a genuine and deep-seated frustration, he pointed in the direction of Washington, D.C., and said, "If they just hadn't taken prayer out of school!"

I started to agree and then it occurred to me that if Christian parents taught their children the importance of prayer before every meal (and every class), prayer would still be in school. If Christian parents encouraged their children that God answers their prayers, students would be praying for every sick friend and teacher. God would be glorified!

Only Christians have the power to take prayer out of school. Depending on the government to keep it there is submitting to the wrong authority. Pointing our fingers at the government, or any other part of society, is blame-shifting. It is all a bunch of bad thinking and we do not think twice about it. So, let's pause a moment and consider what the Holy Bible says.

> *But God forbid that I should boast except in the cross of our Lord Jesus Christ, by whom the world has been crucified to me, and I to the world (Galatians 6:14).*

> *But God, who is rich in mercy, because of His great love with which He loved us, even when we were dead in trespasses, made us alive together with Christ (by grace you have been saved), and raised us up together, and made us sit together in the heavenly places in Christ Jesus… Ephesians 2:4-6*

God Himself, through the cross and the life of Jesus Christ, has separated us from the world. He has seated us at His right hand. The world has no power over the Christian who will just say no. As it is with the Devil, simple resistance wins the day.

This is not to suggest Satan and the world are forces to be ignored; both are known enemies of mankind, attacking us on a continual basis. Consequently, much has been written and preached on the dangers of their deceptions. We have all the reconnaissance and battle strategy we could ever hope for. Indeed, we have no excuse for the way the enemies of God are oppressing and overwhelming the church. The problem is our ignorance of the enemy that lies within.

Satan and the world would not celebrate one victory against a Christian without a hidden ally in the camp. The carnal mind grants, perhaps even orchestrates, their entry and influence. Indeed, the carnal mind is much more responsible for the evil in our lives than we have imagined.

The carnal mind is enemy #1.

The carnal mind has been our greatest enemy all along. Not only does it reside within the camp, mostly hidden from our observation, but we have given it the place of trusted advisor. We regularly turn to our carnal mind for solutions and reasoning about one thing or another. Furthermore, the carnal mind has ready access to whisper fears and false hopes into our souls. It leverages *ego* and *id* to maintain control and influence.

> *But each one is tempted when he is drawn away by his own [carnal] desires and enticed. Then, when desire has conceived, it gives birth to sin; and sin, when it is full-grown, brings forth death (James 1:14-15).*

The first step in addressing a problem is recognizing one exists. If you can answer yes to these questions, you are on your way to overcoming the enemy that lies within.

- Are you beginning to recognize the carnal mind as an enemy?
- Have you noticed the contrast between humanistic worship of the mind and the opinion of Scripture regarding its treachery?
- Do you now respect the threat our carnal mind represents?

Satan and the world work with our carnal mind to inhibit our relationship with God and conform us to their evil ways. Now get this: together, they form an alliance more destructive than either would be separately. Even now they are working hard to minimize your consideration of the danger. Please do not let that happen. Fight back!

But be doers of the word, and not hearers only, deceiving yourselves (James 1:22).

Take Some Time to Challenge Your Thinking

The remainder of this chapter will encourage and challenge you to reconsider the way you think, and inspect just how much of your carnal mind distracts and deceives you. Be suspicious!

Revival from God's Perspective

"All authority has been given to Me in heaven and on earth. Go therefore and make disciples of all the nations, baptizing them in the name of the Father and of the Son and of the Holy Spirit, teaching them to observe all things that I have commanded you; and lo, I am with you always, even to the end of the age." Matthew 28:18-20

For most Christians, Pentecost was the day the Holy Spirit "came in power" upon those who were obediently waiting—a correct but limited and self-centered perspective. Indeed, much of the Church relates Pentecost more to what God gave to us than what He desires from us.

What if Pentecost is about something else; not something different, but something additionally and much more important to the kingdom of God? Have you ever wondered why God chose the Festival of Weeks for the promised coming of the Holy Spirit? Have you ever considered His perspective of Pentecost? Have you ever considered what was in it for Him?

The Festival of Weeks was one of the three great celebrations of the Jewish year; given by God for "*a new grain offering to the LORD*" (Leviticus 23:15-21), "*the firstfruits of wheat harvest*"

(Exodus 34:22). It was—and still is—about the harvest. Is it possible that Pentecost is as much about the harvest of souls for God's kingdom as it is about what we have been given?

The Festival of Weeks was also the time of commemoration for the giving of the Law to Moses. In Jeremiah 31:33, we learn God intends to write His law on our hearts. We know from John 14:26, the Holy Spirit is our teacher. Is it possible Pentecost, from God's perspective, is as much about our "teaching them to observe all that I have commanded" as what we personally receive from the Holy Spirit?

Many in the church are crying out for revival in America; for an outpouring of the Holy Spirit. Why? I can't help but wonder if our subconscious hope is for the return of "the good old days"—days when Christians were respected, protected, and comfortable. Is that what God is after? Could it be that God is waiting for us to align our purpose with His perspective? Should we not be more focused on the desires of His heart: His glory and the advance of His kingdom in the earth?

Just something to think about.

Three Questions for Chaotic Days

If we are not careful, chaos will drive us to carnal reasoning and the resultant carnal response. The best defense is a good offense. Our best offense against the wiles of our carnal mind is the process of faith (more on this later). That process is dependent on an intimate relationship with God, through our Lord Jesus Christ.

> *For everyone who asks receives, and he who seeks finds, and to him who knocks it will be opened (Luke 11:10).*

Behold, I stand at the door and knock. If anyone hears My voice and opens the door, I will come in to him and dine with him, and he with Me (Revelation 3:20).

That the door of intimacy with the Lord opens both ways is an interesting and powerfully encouraging matter. He desires our intimacy like a groom for his bride. Truly, nothing but our reluctance stands in the way.

Recognizing that intimacy requires conversation, let me suggest three conversation starters for your time with God:

Lord Jesus, what are you saying?

Holy Spirit, what are you doing?

Father God, what are you after?

There is an assumption behind these questions: God is after something; He is trying to do something to get what He is after, and, He is willing to tell us all we need to know. God is using this season of chaos (like so many others) to prepare His children for a season of opportunity that is likely beyond our imagination.

It is critically important to recognize that our carnal mind will try to jump in and answer these questions. Barring that, it will work to distract us from hearing and to disprove what we hear. This requires practiced discipline—namely, taking every thought captive to the obedience of Christ, not depending on carnal weapons to make sense of what we hear (2 Corinthians 10:4-5).

Know Your Babylon

And I heard another voice from heaven saying, "Come out of [Babylon], my people, lest you share in her sins, and lest you receive of her plagues." Revelation 18:4

What is this Babylon of the Revelation? Some see it as a real city, the capital of the Antichrist's new world order at the end of the age (the early church thought it was Rome). Others see Babylon as a symbol of sinful humanity and its capacity for self-delusion, pride, and depravity. This would include the systems of this world—government, education, entertainment, etc.—which war against the kingdom of God.

I am encouraged to ask a more important question:

What is this Babylon to you?

What wars against the kingdom of God in your life?

The voice from God encourages us to come out of Babylon. The Holy Spirit draws us and stands by to guide us outside the camp to Jesus, to bear and share His reproach.

Therefore let us go forth to Him, outside the camp, bearing His reproach. For here we have no continuing city, but we seek the one to come (Hebrews 13:13-14).

This journey out of Babylon and into the city of God passes through a narrow gate and down a difficult road (Matthew 7:14). Jesus encourages us to strive to enter through the narrow gate, for many will seek to enter and will not be able (Luke 13:24).

As much as our carnal minds would like to convince us otherwise, we must at some point move from seeking to enter, to striving. Seeking and striving are not the same. The seeker-friendly church and its message may serve some purpose, but it alone will leave untold numbers standing at the gate, wondering if there is more or deceived and camped out, only to be surprised when the books are opened.

God bless you with grace and courage for the narrow gate and difficult road—out of Babylon and into His eternal city.

Conclusion

There are dozens of different ways Christians should be thinking differently. Hopefully, the small sampling provided here has encouraged you toward repentance (i.e., changing the way you think) and a desire for deliverance from some of the more sinister deceptions and captivating distractions. It will be a great advantage in the chaos to have developed a bit of paradigm flexibility and increased dependence on the mind of Christ.

CHAPTER 5

Thinking About America and the Church that Resides Here

To profit from this chapter, some will need to put down their sensitivity to offense. It will help to separate our thinking as a natural citizen of a physical nation from our thinking about the spiritual and physical church that resides here. As much as we may love the former, it is under the sway of the Evil One, it is passing away, and it is not our home. The latter is the Body and future Bride of Christ, a theocracy, and a training ground for a kingdom of holy priests.

Be encouraged, it will not harm you to read what follows. However, dismissing it out-of-hand may leave you ill-prepared when the storms are raging. Many Christians around the world and throughout history have been surprised and devastated when their country became their persecutor. The best way to prepare for such eventualities is to ensure we are thinking rightly about the nations of this world and the heavenly kingdom that has come to militarily transform it.

Adulterers and adulteresses! Do you not know that friendship with the world is enmity with God? Whoever therefore wants to be a friend of the world makes himself an enemy of God (James 4:4).

If you were of the world, the world would love its own. Yet because you are not of the world, but I chose you out of the world, therefore the world hates you (John 15:19).

But now they desire a better, that is, a heavenly country. Therefore God is not ashamed to be called their God, for He has prepared a city for them (Hebrews 13:16).

The way we think about the United States of America and the church that resides here is becoming ever more important. An important question is coming to the foreground. In this day, can we give our hearts' allegiance to both America and the kingdom of God? Only when we come to understand the relationship and dichotomy between of the kingdom of God and America can we rightly assess the value and danger of our patriotism.

Many of America's values and beliefs have become contrary to those in the kingdom of God. Two of the most damaging are the spirit of independence and the belief that man has the right to establish his own rule. Without God, the tensions between the two kingdoms become unmanageable. The United State of America is swiftly becoming an example and object lesson in this regard.

As God is removed from our society, the values and beliefs contrary to His kingdom will become stronger, and more humanistic. The independent spirit will devolve into a spirit of anarchy; while the belief in man-centered rule, driven by the thirst for power and control, will become oligarchy and tyranny. The former will give excuse and purpose to the latter, and vice-versa.

Between those determined to rule and those refusing it are the masses who have decided the state is better resourced to feed, protect, secure, entertain, and govern than the God who created them. A great deception has come upon us. The evil day is at hand. It is time we submitted to the searching of our hearts by God (Psalm 139:23-24). We must rethink the way we think about our nation.

Two Kingdoms and Many Nations

There are two kingdoms and many nations. The nations of this world lie under the power of the Evil One. The dominion of Satan over this world and its nations is convincingly communicated in the Scriptures.

> *And the devil said to Him, "All this authority I will give You, and their glory; for this has been delivered to me, and I give it to whomever I wish." (Luke 4:6).*

> *And you He made alive, who were dead in trespasses and sins, in which you once walked according to the course of this world, according to the prince of the power of the air, the spirit who now works in the sons of disobedience (Ephesians 2:1-2).*

> *But even if our gospel is veiled, it is veiled to those who are perishing, whose minds the god of this age has blinded, who do not believe, lest the light of the gospel of the glory of Christ, who is the image of God, should shine on them (2 Corinthians 4:3-4).*

The United States of America (and every other nation) lies under the power of Satan. Its leaders and its people may claim to be "One Nation Under God", but claims do not make themselves true. This claim can only be true in as much as America is submitted to the reign of God Almighty. Functioning as a democratic republic, where the rights of individuals is paramount, is a difficult, if not impossible, place to start.

Unbelievers, by their nature, are blinded in their minds by the god of this world. Without a born-again spiritual relationship with God, they have only their naturally limited ability to understand goodness and to be "good" people and citizens of America. Furthermore, they attempt to do so under the power of the god of this world. What should we logically expect as the end result? We have been witnessing the answer to that question and will continue to do so.

As Christians, we have been given free will to live under the authority of the nation that lies under the authority of Satan (e.g., allowing the government to decide whether our kids can pray in school or not), but this is to choose a far lower position and authority than we have been offered and to which we have been redeemed and called. Our rebelliously evil and carnal mind would have us settle for less.

> *Now then, we are ambassadors for Christ, as though God were pleading through us: we implore you on Christ's behalf, be reconciled to God (2 Corinthians 5:20).*

We are ambassadors, representatives of the kingdom of God. We answer to the King right now, and we will answer to Him finally at His judgment seat (2 Corinthians 5:10). We are priests and agents of reconciliation (1 Peter 2:9; 2 Corinthians 5:18). We are born of God (1 John 5:1) to be vessels of His glory and instruments of His righteousness (Romans 6:13). Satan, the world, and our carnal minds have deceived us into accepting a poor and natural life. The tragedies of our choices are heartbreaking!

This nation we call America has distracted and deceived us with its "Dream". We, the citizens of the Light, have become a subculture, imprisoned by a life of gray compromise. We have stepped down from our seat in heavenly places (Ephesians 2:6), we have left the Promised Kingdom for the leeks and slavery of Egypt, and we have embraced the Babylon that will be utterly destroyed in the end (or perhaps sooner, in our case).

It is time we came out of the world and stood steadfast in our allegiance to the kingdom of God and its King.

Strong Words for American Christians

The nostalgia many Christian Americans hold of a once predominantly Christian nation is a corporate deception. An objective assessment reveals a country founded through rebellion that embraced slavery and the genocide of its native people. Labeling these historical facts as "America bashing" simply perpetuates the deception. History is what history was.

Current conditions are equally difficult to acknowledge. Two examples come to mind: The United States of America is the largest producer of pornography in the world, and responsible for the reported death of 75 million defenseless babies within our borders and the export of this murderous practice all over the world. Tragically, Christians in this country refused to be God's light and weapons of righteousness against these practices. We have instead become complicit and involved.

Truly, the United States of America has been one of the greatest nations in all of history—from a worldly perspective. Arguably, America has been the world's lone empire for most of the last seventy-five years. Christians like to claim God established this great nation for His purposes, but isn't that true for every government, small and great (Romans 13:1)?

We should ask ourselves: Why did God establish America and bless her with so much? When God formed this nation, He did so to protect the church He was planting here. He had great plans for those who would trust and obey Him; and He accomplished many great things through the church in America. That is something for which we can be grateful (and proud, if you like). God has also used America to overcome evil and improve countless lives all over the globe.

But let's be honest with ourselves, and allow the truth to make us free. Regrettably, the church has become deceived. The wall God provided has become the idol of God's people. Think about it. How many in the church look to America for security, governance, and prosperity? God did not bless America so His people could become rich like the world, while aborting babies and divorcing spouses at the same rate as our godless neighbors. We have compromised ourselves!

Christians like to blame the world (particularly Washington, D.C.) for the ills of society. We do so with a plank in our eye. We have become sub-cultured hypocrites. Fortunately, God has not given up on us.

The church in America stands at a crossroad. Romans 12:2 provides the signpost. One road leads to further conformity; the other to transformation. The time for loitering around has long passed. The chaos of the 2020s will force a decision and compel every Christian down one road or the other. Those who will not strive to enter into God's kingdom will likely find themselves back on the road that leads to destruction.

Reflections on the Prophecy of Haggai

The book of Haggai is a very short book; just two chapters. For such a short read, it has much to say about God's attitude toward His people during times of warning and judgment. With that in mind, I encourage you to consider the following; and I encourage you to hear for yourself what the Father is saying to you and those in your spheres of influence.

Haggai was a prophet sent by God to encourage the rebuilding of the temple in 520 B.C. To understand the importance of Haggai's message, we must first recognize God's temple in the New Covenant context is the body of Christ, the church. Therefore, the prophecy of Haggai applies to the wife of Christ making herself ready (Revelation 19:7) and God's answer to His Son's prayer for our unity (John 17:23).

Some would equate "rebuilding" with "revival". I would not argue with them, except to say true revival is not an event, but a process—a process whereby we are transformed into the image of the glory of the Lord (2 Corinthians 3:18), and are built up into the measure of the stature of the fullness of Christ (Ephesians 4:13).

Regardless of what you call it, the main point is this: Proper work on the temple of God has stopped (or slowed considerably), and God is not happy about it. Judgment is coming to the Church in America. So, please take out your Bible, turn to Haggai, and ask the Holy Spirit to give you wisdom and revelation in its reading.

Who will build the House of the LORD?

Chapter 1, verses 1-11: The people of God have decided it is not time to build the LORD's spiritual house. They have been too busy working on their own physical abodes. Their own possessions are more important to them than the desire of God for a temple that will give Him pleasure and glory. Ironically, their focus on physical provision has resulted in their poverty. Their possessions have come to nothing, at God's hand.

God warns them to "Consider your ways!" This is a fair warning for Christian leaders today. Jesus Christ is building His church; and He is doing it His Father's way. Man's ways for doing God's work will always come short of His intention. Many times, it is a sign of rebellion.

As we prepare for the storm that is coming, these verses challenge us with a question: Where will I invest the lion's share of my time, resources, and energy? Will I focus on protecting my possessions, or will I learn and follow His ways for building the body of Christ?

Verses 12-15: Here we discover the remnant of God: Those that obey the LORD and fear His presence. In response, God stirs up their spirit to work on His spiritual house. The remnant are those who respond humbly to God's warning; in obedience to His reign.

God Rewards the Temple Builders

Chapter 2, verses 1-5: Approximately one month later, the word of the LORD comes again; this time with encouragement. Though the temple they are building appears less than the original, God is more interested in them remaining strong in the work they have been given. He affirms the presence of His Spirit among them; and encourages them not to fear. They are to press on with the work regardless of the troubles and trials that will come against them.

Verses 6-9: Here God explains His ultimate purpose for the temple His people are working on (remember, in the New Testament context, this is the body of Christ). God is preparing to shake the nations (see Hebrews 12:25-29) to get their attention; that they would see His temple filled with His glory. In fact, the glory of the latter will be greater than the original; and it will be a house of peace.

This reminds me of Matthew 5:16: *Let your light so shine before men that they see your good work and glorify your Father in heaven.* Note that each use of "your" is plural. The glory of the Father is radiated from the body of Christ. Our light is the life of Christ (John 1:4). Therefore, our temple building work includes the increase of the image of the glory of the Lord in those within our spheres of influence. In other words, we are to be making disciples of the Lord Jesus Christ (Matthew 28:18-20).

Verses 10-14: At this point, the LORD interjects another warning. Those who mix the holy with the common are defiled; along with their work and their offering. We are to be in the world, but not of it. What does this mean? How about: *No one engaged in warfare entangles himself with the affairs of this life, that he may please him who enlisted him as a soldier* (2 Timothy 2:4)? The church Christ is building is to be a counter-culture, not a subculture. What do your spheres of influence look like? The world, or the body of Christ?

Verses 15-17: God reminds His people of the warning they failed to heed. The church has been warned of her idolatry with the American Dream at least twice in this century. Generally speaking, they have had little effect. We have continued to pursue our own prosperity; at the expense of God's desires (i.e., His reign, habitation, and intimacy, over and with us). How much longer will He permit our rebellion?

Verses 18-19: This is perhaps the greatest encouragement of Haggai. The people of God did not have to complete the temple to begin receiving God's blessing. They only had to begin the work. Surely, together, you and your spheres of influence can lay the foundation for fellowship. Try Acts 2:42 as a start. Do so, and the blessings of the LORD will come.

Verses 20-23: In response to the leader's faithfulness, God made him "like a signet ring". The signet ring is a sign of authority and rule. Like the good and faithful servant in the Parable of the Talents, the Master will make you the ruler of much more than you can ask or imagine.

This is the desire of our Father's heart: to see His people blessed in supernatural ways. I hope and pray you will commit yourself to building His temple—the body of Christ—during this critical time in the history of the church.

The Need for Prophecy in this Season

There are those among us whose hearts can discern between the true and the false, whose spiritual sense of smell enables them to detect the spurious afar off, who have the blessed gift of knowing. Let such as these arise and be heard. Who knows but the Lord may yet return and leave a blessing behind Him (Tozer, 1991).

There has never been a greater need for the gift of prophecy in the church than the season we are now facing. This gift, in all its forms, has been dismissed and abused, shunned, and neglected.

But to each one of us grace was given according to the measure of Christ's gift. Therefore He says:

"When He ascended on high,
He led captivity captive,
And gave gifts to men."

...And He Himself gave some to be apostles, some
prophets, some evangelists, and some pastors and teachers,
for the equipping of the saints for the work of ministry,
for the edifying of the body of Christ (Ephesians 4:7-11).

Prophets have been given by Christ for ministry to the church and beyond. Who in their right mind would refuse such a gift? Prophets are given for our good!

There are diversities of gifts, but the same Spirit ... But
the manifestation of the Spirit is given to each one for the
profit of all ... to another prophecy ... But one and the
same Spirit works all these things, distributing to each one
individually as He wills (1 Corinthians 12:4-11).

Pursue love, and desire spiritual gifts, but especially that
you may prophesy ... he who prophesies speaks edifica-
tion and exhortation and comfort to men (1 Corinthians
14:1-3)

I was not raised in a denomination that talked much about prophecy; and I recognize I am not an expert. But this I know, prophecy is a gift of Jesus Christ and the Holy Spirit. It is time we searched it out seriously for our personal preparation and for the edification, exhortation, and comfort of those in our spheres of influence.

As a start, let me offer a brief perspective on the ways prophecy has been offered as a gift to the children of God.

The Prophecy of Scripture: The prophets of old had much to say about God's purpose, plans, and expectations for His people. I have been reading Jeremiah and I can't help but think it contains a warning for the American Church (check out Chapter 11). Jeremiah has been a difficult book to read. The Holy Spirit has not allowed me to read it as an historical account. He has not allowed me to project it on a "them". He has continually reminded me that it was written not only as a warning to those who would come after, but to me as an individual child of God. That is a good thing.

The Prophets of Today: Jesus Himself gave prophets to the Church; that we might become His fully mature body (Ephesians 4:7-11). It is reasonable to assume—since our maturity has not been accomplished—that prophets are with us today. It is important we pray for God to give them courage and the faith to speak the truth to the body of Christ; and we pray for the grace to discern those that are falsely speaking, "Peace, peace."

The Personal Gift: We are encouraged to desire the Holy Spirit's gift of prophecy (1 Corinthians 14:1). This is both foretelling (God's word for the future) and forth-telling (God's truth for this generation). What is common to both is the power and surety of the message. If the Holy Spirit has determined to give you this gift, you must not neglect it; for your neglect will grieve Him and harm the body of Christ.

Please note this is simply a suggested starting point; not the final answer for you and your faith community. You must search out the gifts of prophecy for yourself.

I close with a specific word to Christian leaders: God has positioned you to impact your spheres of influence for His kingdom. This is one area of particular importance to you.

You have been given a platform. You are responsible for using it; and you will answer to the Master when He returns. Pursue prophecy.

Obeying the New Covenant

> *But now He has obtained a more excellent ministry, inasmuch as He is also Mediator of a better covenant, which was established on better promises. For if that first covenant had been faultless, then no place would have been sought for a second. Because finding fault with them, He says: "Behold, the days are coming, says the LORD, when I will make a new covenant with the house of Israel and with the house of Judah..." (Hebrews 8:6-8 [from Jeremiah 31:31]).*

We have broken our covenant with the LORD. Given God's reaction to Israel and Judah over their disobedience (in Jeremiah, Isaiah, Ezekiel, etc.), it is frightening (word chosen carefully) to think about the consequences for us. The New Covenant is so much more than the Old; and to those who have been given much, much is expected.

Jeremiah (via Hebrews) challenges us with two important questions:

1. What is the New Covenant?
2. What does obedience to it look like?

Before you give the quick answer, please consider the following passages (you might also want to read the first twelve chapters of Jeremiah):

> *And it shall come to pass that whoever calls on the name of the Lord shall be saved (Acts 2:21).*

For God so loved the world that He gave His only begotten Son, that whoever believes in Him should not perish but have everlasting life (John 3:16).

… if you confess with your mouth the Lord Jesus and believe in your heart that God has raised Him from the dead, you will be saved (Romans 10:9).

Not everyone who says to Me, "Lord, Lord," shall enter the kingdom of heaven, but he who does the will of My Father in heaven. Many will say to Me in that day, "Lord, Lord, have we not prophesied in Your name, cast out demons in Your name, and done many wonders in Your name?" And then I will declare to them, "I never knew you; depart from Me, you who practice lawlessness!" (Matthew 7:21-23).

The New Covenant, which God has ordained, requires more of us than many of us have been taught. Cherry-picking select verses, we have allowed ourselves to disbelieve or remain ignorant of the full context of Scripture. We do so to our peril.

Calling on the name of the Lord means more than calling out His name and more than tacking "in Jesus' name" to our prayers. The same can be said for confession with our mouth in Jesus' lordship. "Whoever believes in Him" is more than raising a hand and saying a prayer. It is more than conversion. The one who believes unto salvation "does the will of my Father in heaven". This is the New Covenant.

How did this happen to us? How could we miss such a clear and sobering warning? My humble opinion: our disbelief and/or ignorance is proof the church has sub-cultured itself to the American way of life. Convenience is king and marketing-savvy religious organizations have learned the least costly gospel draws the most people. Like the world around us, we have become arrogant to think we can change the terms of the New Covenant. And we refuse to think about the prospects, lest we realize the profound silliness of it all.

It feels like I am stating the obvious, but here goes: the deception that has come over the church in America is much greater than we perceive. We, each one of us, need eyes to see, and ears to hear. We need the truth which will make us free. We need courage to confess and reject our idols. We need to renew our vows. We need the prophets.

Conclusion

As we close out this section—to move on to the restoration of our houses—please prayerfully consider the following inspection questions. Receiving an honest report from our heavenly Inspector is the goal here. You will likely have to force your carnal mind to hold its excuses, blame-shifting, and attempts at distraction.

1. Who or what currently provides you the greatest sense of security?
2. Where do you first turn when sickness finds you or those you love?
3. How would you explain the difference between your love of country and your love of God? Would you be satisfied with your answer?
4. Why do you love your country? How many of those things are important to God? How many of those things should instead be found in God?
5. Would you give up your rights as an American citizen to become a kingdom ambassador to a worldly nation?
6. Who is responsible for defending your right to life?

7. What does it mean to you to be in this world but not of it? In which part of your life is this question most difficult to answer?

Again, do not be discouraged; an incredibly small number will be happy with their answers. Challenging inspection has been the necessary first step toward the restoration of our house— that we might securely abide there during storms and chaos. Truly, it is a gift and grace of God. As often as is necessary, exercise His prescription for confession and cleansing:

> *If we confess our sins, He is faithful and just to forgive us our sins and to cleanse us from all unrighteousness (1 John 1:9).*

Our loving Father, King, and Comforter is waiting to hear our cry for help.

> *Then they cry out to the LORD in their trouble,*
> *And He brings them out of their distresses.*
> *He calms the storm,*
> *So that its waves are still.*
> *Then they are glad because they are quiet;*
> *So He guides them to their desired haven*
> *(Psalm 107:28-30).*

They have promised to respond.

A Pause for Encouragement

House inspections typically induce anxiety for the owner-seller. We never know what the professionals will discover, but we suspect it will be more than we imagined. On the other hand, the potential new inhabitants depend on the inspection to protect them from purchasing a money-pit. Once again, our perspective in this process must be guarded and maintained.

My family had a house fire that turned into an adventure (more on that later), ending in the purchase of my wife's dream home (her words). The purchase was not without risk; our new home had been sitting unoccupied for two years and the deal included an "as is" stipulation. Fortunately, the insurance company was willing to pay for the most obvious restorations. However, now ten years later, we are starting to discover the results of shoddy workmanship that will have to be addressed. We should have had a formal inspection; who knows, the insurance company might have paid for more.

With that real life analogy in mind, we encourage you to take full advantage of the inspection step. If necessary, stop, go back, and allow God to lovingly reveal any points of foundation weakness or shoddy construction that jeopardizes the strength of your house.

Those who have welcomed and heeded the heavenly Inspector are now encouraged to move quickly to His restoration. As the permanent resident of our house, anticipating severe storms and chaos, we hear wisdom calling us to God's restorative work. The quicker we address the damage the better, for the storms have already begun!

Things like this—God working in us to will and to do for His good pleasure—always appear more difficult and challenging on the front end. We must allow God's encouragement to carry the day. The nation of Israel learned that lesson the hard way when God first invited them into the Promised Land. They discovered postponing the required restoration would only increase the cost. Losing a house to the storms will be just as devastating to us and those dependent on our courageous obedience.

Encouragement—the act of putting courage in—is truly something we all need in this season. Courage is contagious; it can be drawn from others, and it can be shared. Perhaps the greatest courage needed in this hour is for commitment to the LORD's way, trusting Him to bring to pass whatever He desires (Psalm 37:5).

One of the LORD's more difficult ways is waiting. As the pandemic of 2020 began, most of us voluntarily sequestered ourselves in our homes. Many I spoke with believed God was trying to get our attention, drawing us closer to Him for rest, reset, and renewal, in preparation for the kingdom-advancing opportunities the coming storms would provide. Since then, the chaos of economic crisis and the lawlessness gripping this country has threatened to distract and draw us from God's presence and peace.

Therefore, in the midst of moving on to restoration, we must be careful to also continue waiting for the LORD.

For since the beginning of the world
Men have not heard nor perceived by the ear,
Nor has the eye seen any God besides You,
Who acts for the one who waits for Him (Isaiah 64:4).

God is not waiting for us to act as much as He is waiting on us to wait. Now, this waiting is not procrastination, but a patience which ensures we are adequately prepared to participate in His good work when He says, "Go!" The tension we feel between waiting and going fosters an expectation and obedience, and develops within us the focused attention on the LORD we will need to withstand the storms and navigate the chaos they produce.

Furthermore, be encouraged by the words of Jesus for the end of the Age:

Behold, I stand at the door and knock. If anyone hears
My voice and opens the door, I will come in to him and
dine with him, and he with Me. To him who overcomes I
will grant to sit with Me on My throne, as I also overcame
and sat down with My Father on His throne (Revelation 3:20-21).

The Lord desires our time and attention so much that He—the King of kings—is knocking on our door. For heaven's sake (and your own), take advantage of Jesus' offer. The invitation is real; the promises, steadfast and eternal. As a dear friend once said to me, "God is not hiding from us."

Finally, consider this closing encouragement:

Serving the King,
Who you love and admire,

Is neither burden nor responsibility;
It is opportunity and privilege.

Instruments are useless,
Until they are put to good use.
They lay in the dark drawer,
Lonely,
Until the Master selects them,
For His good work.

The most useful tools,
Are the ones placed out,
Within easy reach.
They fit the Master's hand,
And His hand fits them.

God bless you with peace in the storms, courage in the chaos, and patience for His presence.

Step Two – Restore

CHAPTER 6

Restoring Our Faith in God's Faithfulness

Commit your way to the Lord,
Trust also in Him,
And He shall bring it to pass.
He shall bring forth your righteousness as the light,
And your justice as the noonday.
Psalm 37:5

If you have made it this far, you may be surprised to read I am excited and hopeful for the church, including that portion of her that resides in America. I often have to remind myself of this fact, but it is nevertheless true.

There are two reasons for my hopefulness. First, I believe the Bride of the Lamb is making herself ready, and she will be perfectly beautiful (Revelation 19:7-8). Secondly, I believe the storms and chaos God is allowing or creating give testimony to His continued longsuffering and persistence for His Son and His Son's bride. The New Covenant consummates in the relationship God has been after since the beginning of time.

Our Father in heaven is the ultimate refuge and encouragement. The houses who stand are really just vessels and instruments of His mercy and grace. Without His Son, we can do absolutely nothing; abiding in Him, we will bear much fruit during the storms (John 15:5).

So, though the tone to this point may suggest otherwise, this book is not written from a desperate heart. Please understand this: the storms and chaos will create great opportunities for the church to reclaim her identity and character. The storms and chaos will create great opportunities for evangelism and disciple making. Please, please, please, allow (or force) your mind to think this way, that you might recognize and leverage every opportunity God draws or drives your way.

One additional word of explanation for this section: Scripture—particularly the New Testament—has much more to say about what we should believe and how we should think than the work we are to be doing. The good works of faith follow repentance, hearing and believing God's word (Romans 10:17), and our obedience to His word (Romans 16:26). We must get our thinking and believing right before we go off doing stuff.

Consequently, this section will continue to challenge your paradigms and beliefs. Let it! Use what you learn to encourage and edify others—that is, "go make disciples." Do not worry, the Holy Spirit will prompt you to do things with and for others when the time is right. Timing and ministry targets are best heard from Him. Do them exactly as He commands! Know He is repairing, restoring, and strengthening your houses (i.e., yours and theirs).

It Will be Good for Us

The spiritual restoration we are suggesting here is something we, as Christians, should have been doing anyway. There is nothing new under the sun. The church today is suffering in many of the same ways it has suffered over the past 2000+ years (e.g., division, apathy, worldliness). The solutions, though daunting, are unchanged (e.g., surrender, die to self, love God and love others, sacrifice, serve).

The entire New Testament was written during a time of chaos. Indeed, God used each of the main characters (e.g., Jesus, Peter, Paul) as His instruments in creating the chaos that surrounded them. When God manifests Himself, chaos ensues. Chaos is not only normal for a Christian; it is a sign of God's presence. In the chaos, the part of us that belongs to God has access to the peace of God that transcends all understanding (Philippians 4:7). Still, we must allow the chaos to test and purify; we must allow it to shake out that which shall not remain (Hebrews 12:25-29).

However, something is significantly different for the church during this season: a growing sense of urgency. Whether from those who sense a storm is coming, or from those who have experienced the slow but growing decline of the church's influence in society, those who will take their heads out of the sand and truly consider the situation will sense the growing urgency.

This urgency has created, and will continue to create, a new type of opportunity. As the American idol continues to disappoint its worshippers (Christians included), the light of the life of Christ will be seen in those who have built their houses on the solid foundation of hearing and doing what Jesus says (Matthew 7:24-25). Those who will shore up their foundation will become houses of refuge in the storm.

When chaos finds its way into our lives, it creates a tension between our desire to maintain current normalcy (aka, comfort zone) and our finding the new normal which God is trying to work in us and through us.

But we all, with unveiled face, beholding as in a mirror the glory of the Lord, are being transformed into the same image from glory to glory, just as by the Spirit of the Lord (2 Corinthians 3:18).

Not that I have already attained, or am already perfected; but I press on, that I may lay hold of that for which Christ Jesus has also laid hold of me (Philippians 3:12).

Our carnal mind attempts to inhibit God's work by distracting us and/or dissuading us from the reality that God is up to something. Those who notice themselves focused more on maintaining the status quo than on finding the next level of glory, should immediately suspect their carnal mind and invite the Holy Spirit to renew their thinking (Romans 12:2). Only then will we know the will of God in the chaos.

Furthermore, times like these test our love for others. The love of God for brethren and neighbor is, more than anything else, sacrificial. When our brother or sister is out of work, are we eager to sacrifice in helping to provide for their family? Are we willing to reach out to our neighbor? How do we respond to 1 John 3:17-18?

But whoever has this world's goods, and sees his brother in need, and shuts up his heart from him, how does the love of God abide in him? My little children, let us not love in word or in tongue, but in deed and in truth.

Hopefully, we will not be like the people who lived below a dam, meeting regularly to discuss the cracks, but continuing to live as if the dam would never fail. The foolish man knows what is right, but doesn't take action. The wise man stops investing in what is passing away. We must lay up treasures in

74

heaven. We must buy the truth. May we be found dressed in readiness with our lamp's lit (Luke 12:35).

> *Those who do wickedly against the covenant he shall corrupt with flattery; but the people who know their God shall be strong, and carry out great exploits (Daniel 11:32).*

> *Many shall be purified, made white, and refined, but the wicked shall do wickedly; and none of the wicked shall understand, but the wise shall understand (Daniel 12:10).*

> *And His voice shook the earth then, but now He has promised, saying, "Yet once more I will shake not only the earth, but also the heaven." This expression, "Yet once more," denotes the removing of those things which can be shaken, as of created things, so that those things which cannot be shaken may remain. Therefore, since we receive a kingdom which cannot be shaken, let us show gratitude, by which we may offer to God an acceptable service with reverence and awe; for our God is a consuming fire (Hebrews 12:26-29, NASB).*

Our restoration depends on our willingness to embrace the storm as something God has allowed or created for the church; and something that will be good for us. The storm is for the church, because the church is for the Son. The storm will be exactly what is needed to purify the Bride; nothing more or less. The sooner we recognize the judgment of God, the better off we will be. God's desire for His children is clear:

1. Confession and repentance;
2. Reverent surrender;

3. Laying aside every weight in marriage, family, church, etc.;
4. Radical obedience; and,
5. Purity and radical holiness.

The storms will shake individuals, church fellowships, and denominations (Hebrews 12:27). There will be a falling away (2 Thessalonians 2:1-4). This is one of the more sobering things to me. Still, it will be good for us. There will be a renewal of the remnant, for the shaking will test and strengthen their abiding in Christ, His word, and His love.

Storms and fires are necessary to bring life to forests that have been poorly attended. We need to recognize why the storm is needed. Now is the time to begin removing what does not belong. It will be less painful to do so before the storms and God's purifying fire come.

Don't Let the Pain Stop You

Storms tend to inflict pain—emotional, physical, and mental pain. The pain of loss due to poor foundations or shoddily built structures. The pain of watching a loved one suffer from poor decisions. The pain that comes with having something or someone who does not belong removed from our life. This will be our pain, and the pain of those in our spheres of influence.

Whatever the cause and nature of the pain, God has promised two things:

1. He will be in it with us (Hebrews 13:5).
2. He will work it to our good (Romans 8:28).

Or course, this is only true for those who are prepared to face the pain with faith and courage. I recently learned this lesson while riding my bicycle.

At my advanced age, riding regularly ends with a lot of pain in the legs (no pain, no gain). This time, the pain began less than one mile into the ride. I had sensations in my left leg unlike any I have experienced. It started in my knee and moved from there to my thigh and calf; almost like a double cramp. It was weird.

My first thought was to turn back. My second thought was the same. However, the weather was perfectly beautiful, so I pressed on. Eventually the pain subsided and I finished the ride as planned.

Like many of you, when something strange like this happens, I have learned to ask the Lord, "What's up with that?" The answer I got back was:

"Pain will stop you… if you let it."

The days ahead promise to be painful in one way or another, as our houses are tested and we are shaken. Dying to self is a painful process. Furthermore, we are all being transformed into the image of the glory of the Lord, and transformation can be a painful process. Just ask the caterpillar.

Whatever the pain, we must not let it stop us—stealing our adventure and the desire of our heart. The Lord is leading us, under the Father's protection, in step with the Holy Spirit. The other side of our transformations will be glorious. We will know the Master's pleasure.

Receive this encouragement: find those who will encourage you through the pain; and find the ones you are to encourage. Find community and you will find courage. Be strong in the Lord, and in the power of His might (Ephesians 6:10). In your weakness, you are made strong (2Corinthians 12:10).

Set Your Mind for Chaos

> *If then you were raised with Christ, seek those things which are above, where Christ is, sitting at the right hand of God. Set your mind on things above, not on things on the earth. For you died, and your life is hidden with Christ in God (Colossians 3:1-3).*

Knowing God is sovereign, we can confidently say He creates or allows the storms and chaos that find their way into our lives. We also believe He works **all things** to the good of those who love Him and are called to His purpose (Romans 8:28). How we respond to chaos makes more difference in our lives, and the lives of those in our spheres of influence, than we might think or imagine.

Generally speaking, chaos either draws us away from the truth or it serves to focus our attention on what is fundamentally real (i.e., the heavenly perspective). The greater the chaos, the greater the impact in one of these two directions.

Chaos tests the set of our mind. Chaos also gives us the opportunity to practice our resistance to the enemy's distraction and deception. By the way, the enemy I am referring to is our carnal mind—our number one enemy. Scripture makes it clear neither Satan nor the world can influence a child of God (James 4:7; Galatians 6:14) unless they are allowed to do so. Our carnal mind opens that door.

78

Most of us have been trained for much of our lives to turn to our carnal mind when chaos invades our lives. This is directly and exactly the opposite of God's intention. When chaos comes, He would have us choose the influence and direction of Christ's mind. Make no mistake about it: We are responsible for that choice.

Choosing submission to the mind of Christ is the way we set our mind on things above. Like any exercise, this practice forms and strengthens our heavenly and eternal mind set. Chaos affords us the opportunity to be transformed by the renewing of our mind, that we might discover the good, acceptable, and perfect will of God for the chaos and life beyond it (Romans 12:2).

God also allows or creates chaos to fashion opportunities for His children to glorify Him through supernatural good works (Matthew 5:16). The possibilities are exceedingly, abundantly above all we can ask or think, according to the power that works in us (Ephesians 3:20).

So, how do we participate with God as He glorifies Himself in chaos? The answer is so simple I feel I must warn you not to dismiss it (that is the intention of your carnal mind). To set our minds on things above—to submit to the mind of Christ in the midst of chaos—we simply begin by bringing our questions to God.

Why are we isolated?

Why am I fearful, or self-protective?

What is my role in this? How can I help?

Should I go there? Should I help that person?

These are just a few examples. Whatever the question, take it to God. He loves talking with His children. Please, please, please, avoid the reasoning of your carnal mind. What seems right to our natural man separates us from the voice of the One who loves us. Presumption inhibits our hearing the word of God. Without that word, we will not have faith for the grace of God that accomplishes the "exceedingly, abundantly above all". Wait on God for the answer. Remember:

> *For from days of old they have not heard or perceived*
> *by ear,*
> *Nor has the eye seen a God besides You,*
> *Who acts in behalf of the one who waits for Him*
> *(Isaiah 64:4).*

God bless you with conviction, courage, opportunity, and grace to set your mind on things above—to seek and find the heavenly perspective.

The Heavenly Perspective

> *He answered and said to them, "Because it has been given*
> *to you to know the mysteries of the kingdom of heaven,*
> *but to them it has not been given... But blessed are your*
> *eyes for they see, and your ears for they hear; for assuredly,*
> *I say to you that many prophets and righteous men desired*
> *to see what you see, and did not see it, and to hear what*
> *you hear, and did not hear it." (Matthew 13:11, 16-17).*

The children of God have been blessed with eyes to see and ears to hear, that we might know the mysteries of the kingdom of heaven. Constrained in our earthly body, we tend to under-estimate this gift and ability. Trusting God in the storms and chaos comes easier when we view them from His perspective.

But God, who is rich in mercy, because of His great love with which He loved us, even when we were dead in trespasses, made us alive together with Christ (by grace you have been saved), and raised us up together, and made us sit together in the heavenly places in Christ Jesus (Ephesians 2:4-6).

Because of His great love, God has saved and **seated us together in the heavenly places** in Christ Jesus. From there, we might enjoy His perspective of all that is going on around us… or we might choose not to. It is our responsibility to observe, process, and respond to our environment and all its activity from the heavenly perspective. Doing so exercises the mind of Christ we have been given (1 Corinthians 2:16).

To lay hold of this grace, we must first believe the heavenly perspective is available, and then we must choose it as an act of our will. Some may hesitate, fearing the temptation of haughtiness. Such a fear should not be ignored. We must not think we are sufficient for these things, but reckon our sufficiency is from God (2 Corinthians 3:5-6). We must remain humble, and allow the Holy Spirit to deal with our flesh—another reason for daily communion with God, who is a consuming fire (Hebrews 12:29).

Indeed, those who know the grace of God from the perspective of God are not concerned with their personal rights, nor easily distracted by injustice done to them. They see beyond these things, into eternity. They have been set free from temporal matters and considerations.

Looking over our circumstances from Christ's perspective provides supernatural breadth and depth, both of the situation and God's intentions for it. We are given insight into motives and masks. We become healing instruments for God's children and deadly weapons against His enemies.

If we truly believe we are children of God, and we truly believe He is sufficient for everything He desires of us, things would be different in our lives and in our spheres of influence. It occurs to me that each one of us should reckon the truth of this at the beginning of every day (and probably many times before its end).

I am moved deep in my soul by the importance of this. It is a transformational matter, an epiphany. The thought of it stirs the desire in my heart to see and engage the world as a child of the perfectly good and loving King. Why would we settle for anything less than the perspective we have been offered and commanded to walk in (2 Peter 1:1-11)?

Beware, it will be easy to accept this as true and not believe it. The hearing of faith must be followed by obedience to the faith for the work of faith to effectually manifest God's grace in and through our being. We must allow the Holy Spirit to truly renew our minds in this matter of our humble and royal estate.

Let us be encouraged: God has put a desire in our hearts for everything He desires of us. If we will surrender, commit our way to Him, and trust in Him, He will bring it to pass. He will bring forth our righteousness as the light, and our justice as the noonday (Psalms 37:4-6).

We must humbly resign ourselves to nothing less than what God has made of us in our rebirth, and nothing more than submitted participation in the good work of the Father, Son, and Holy Spirit. Without Jesus Christ, we can do nothing; yet through Him, we can do all things. His life is all we need.

God bless you with faith and courage to observe, process, and respond to your environment from His perspective. God bless you with the renewal of your mind.

God's Promise, Provision, and Prescription for Peace

> *...and the peace of God, which surpasses all under-standing, will guard your hearts and minds through Christ Jesus (Philippians 4:7).*

The peace of God is supernatural and powerful—even as much as His love, mercy, and grace. Regrettably, many of God's children have succumbed to the fears and anxieties of the world. Restoring our faith in the peace of God which surpasses all understanding is of paramount importance for the storms that will buffet our houses. We will not find the peace God offers—for ourselves and those who have lost their houses—unless we start believing God's promise, provision, and prescription for it.

With that in mind, consider the promise, provision and way of peace offered to every child of God. It starts with the prophecy of His coming.

> *But He was wounded for our transgressions,*
> *He was bruised for our iniquities;*
> *The chastisement for our peace was upon Him,*
> *And by His stripes we are healed (Isaiah 53:5).*

This much quoted verse contains something I had not noticed until recently. Not only was the Messiah to be wounded, bruised, and scourged, but he was also promised as the chastisement **for our peace**. He took on the Father's correction, reproof, and rebuke, that we might have peace through Him.

The LORD God is faithful and trustworthy. He is almighty—able to do all He says. He keeps His promises. That includes the provision of His peace.

> *Therefore, having been justified by faith, **we have peace with God through our Lord Jesus Christ**, through whom also we have access by faith into this grace in which we stand, and rejoice in hope of the glory of God (Romans 5:1-2).*

> *For it pleased the Father that in Him all the fullness should dwell, and by Him to reconcile all things to Himself, by Him, whether things on earth or things in heaven, **having made peace through the blood of His cross** (Colossians 1:19-20).*

It is important to note: The eternal peace we have with God is the provision for our peace in the storms of this life. Maintaining this connection in your heart and mind will bring revelation and power for the peace of God in the midst of the storms.

Now, the peace of the kingdom of God is found and emanates from our King in proportion to His reign in our lives. He has been given all authority in heaven and on earth (Matthew 28:18), so perfect peace is possible.

We must come to understand the proportional relationship between peace and submission to the King's authority. Indeed, the overriding requisite for the peace that surpasses all understanding is His reign.

> *And **let the peace of God rule** in your hearts, to which also you were called in one body; and be thankful (Colossians 3:15).*

Times of turmoil, crisis, and chaos are created or allowed by God to help us align our allegiance to His Son. In doing so, we position ourselves to receive His peace.

God has made Jesus Christ our peace. He has also made a way for His children to find and live in the peace that surpasses all understanding.

> *Rejoice in the Lord always. Again I will say, rejoice! Let your gentleness be known to all men. The Lord is at hand. Be anxious for nothing, but in everything by prayer and supplication, with thanksgiving, let your requests be made known to God; and the peace of God, which surpasses all understanding, will guard your hearts and minds through Christ Jesus (Philippians 4:4-7).*

During a particularly stressful time in my life (a time that included daily panic attacks), the Holy Spirit introduced me to this passage, and trained me to use it as God's recipe for peace and a weapon against the enemy. What Satan intended for evil, God turned to my good.

Here is a general version of the resulting prayer.

> Father in Heaven, I rejoice in Your presence. I rejoice in the promise of Your protection and peace in this circumstance! I surrender to the expression of Your gentleness to everyone involved—even those who appear to be my enemies. I know You are with me in every trial and tribulation. By Your grace, I refuse to be anxious. Thank You for this opportunity to experience and prove Your love. I pray for Your protection and guidance in this situation. I will not be able to persevere without You. I desperately need You. I receive

Your peace and I rest in Your protection, through Your Son; in whose name I pray. Amen.

In closing, let me encourage you to be as specific as you can in your prayer. Pray with the mind of Christ—full of faith and humility. The peace of God will bear witness of His trustworthiness to those in your spheres of influence. They will be encouraged and comforted in your peace. They will be drawn to Him.

Counting the Cost

As we face the potentially painful restoration of our house, our thoughts naturally turn to, "What will it cost me?" There's just no getting around it: God's promises for security and strength are conditional and costly. Indeed, Jesus encourages us to count the cost (Luke 14:25-33). However, we must take care when assessing the cost to do so with the reward in mind. Again, Jesus models the way for us:

> *Therefore we also, since we are surrounded by so great a cloud of witnesses, let us lay aside every weight, and the sin which so easily ensnares us, and let us run with endurance the race that is set before us, looking unto Jesus, the author and finisher of our faith, who for the joy that was set before Him endured the cross, despising the shame, and has sat down at the right hand of the throne of God (Hebrews 12:1-2).*

The enemies of God would have us focus on the cost, that we might abandon God's will and way for our lives. This is another battleground with our carnal mind. At enmity with God, the mind of our flesh would have us perceive and relate to God as oppressor. This is a mindset we must cast down (2 Corinthians 10:5), keeping the promised rewards at the forefront of our mind. As exacting as the conditions may seem, we will discover they do not compare to God's reward for our obedience.

Conditions can be viewed in two opposing ways. We can consider them as responsibilities forced upon us for some desired outcome, or as opportunities for reward. Our mindset in this regard has a great deal to do with our relationship and interaction with the one setting the conditions, as well as our response to them.

A classic example is our view of labor for income. Those who appreciate labor as an opportunity to earn income enjoy their work and make better employees. Persons who feel their labor is forced on them are generally disgruntled workers, slaves to their jobs.

The Father's good pleasure is to give us His kingdom (Luke 12:32). His desire is for a people who will surrender to His reign, welcome His habitation, and enjoy the intimacy of His presence. Recognizing our weak estate, our loving Father has graciously and lavishly provided motivation for pursuing what He is after.

In the battle against our carnal mind's deception and deceit, it helps to fully appreciate the matter of our participation in God's work. He works in us to will and to do for His good pleasure (Philippians 2:13), and without His Son, we can do nothing (John 15:5). "Good works" are God's work. They are created for us to walk in them, not to do them. This alone encourages us to see God's conditions as opportunities.

Isaiah 58 provides a great example of God's way for our participation with Him in His good works. Furthermore, a careful examination of His conditions and rewards reveals the supernatural return-on-investment He lavishes on His children. So, let's take a look.

Isaiah 58 challenges us to think about fasting from a different perspective. For most of my Christian life, my consideration of fasting focused on the method, with a restricted view of the purpose. The food or activity I determined to fast defined the method and (unintentionally) created a performance-oriented activity. In my mind, the purpose was limited to hearing God's voice and/or getting God to do something important.

A close friend and mentor helped me look at Isaiah 58 from a different perspective—to expand my view of fasting in two important ways. First, God has given us fasting as a catalyst for our participation in His good work. Secondly, He has prescribed four very specific purposes for our fasting—things that please Him.

The first of these "condition-reward" couplets serves our purposes here. We will examine the others in Section Three, as they apply to abiding and will provide a convenient reminder of God's way for our participation in the opportunities He encourages.

> *Is this not the fast that I have chosen:*
> *To loose the bonds of wickedness,*
> *To undo the heavy burdens,*
> *To let the oppressed go free,*
> *And that you break every yoke (Isaiah 58:6)?*

This verse sounds much like Jesus' inauguration speech, found in Luke 4:18, "*To proclaim liberty to the captives and recovery of sight to the blind, to set at liberty those who are oppressed…*" And then I am reminded that our King passed on His anointing to us, "*As the Father has sent Me, I also send you*" (John 20:21).

Let's face it, this loosing, undoing, and breaking sounds like a lot of hard work. It certainly adds perspective to Jesus' commission to go and make disciples. One thing I have discovered in fifteen years of ministry to workplace leaders, most need to be set free before they are much use to God. To be honest and transparent, this is truer of myself than I would care to discuss.

And so, we remind ourselves this is opportunity—opportunity to be an instrument of God's liberty for others, while we find it ourselves. The truth will make us free, including the truth we need to participate with God for the freedom He requires.

Walking in spiritual and emotional freedom, we are then capable of more practical endeavors.

> *Is it not to share your bread with the hungry,*
> *And that you bring to your house the poor who are cast out;*
> *When you see the naked, that you cover him,*
> *And not hide yourself from your own flesh (Isaiah 58:7)?*

I confess this verse intimidates me, for it requires a surrender that truly challenges my faith. I want to ask, "What is enough sharing? Is this 'bring to your house the poor' for everyone? Who are these naked? How unhid must I become?"

Some of you will recognize these questions expose the limits of my faith, and serve to inhibit God's answers to them and my subsequent participation in His good works. Is it the same for you? The frustrating thing for me is I know what's required.

> *If anyone wills to do His will, he shall know concerning*
> *the doctrine, whether it is from God or whether I speak*
> *on My own authority. He who speaks from himself seeks*
> *his own glory; but He who seeks the glory of the One who*

sent Him is true, and no unrighteousness is in Him (John 7:17-18).

To know when to share, bring, cover, and not hide, one must will to do His will. I believe this is true for me, but can one know for sure who has not been tested? Most of us are born with test-avoidance built in, and excuses are easy to come by. Again, our carnal mind must be resisted.

Do we see these conditions for God's gracious promises as opportunity or burden? Most people have sense enough to pursue opportunities, not ignore or avoid them. Perhaps that is the test.

As hard as this has been to write (and I suspect hard to read), the privilege to encourage with God's promised reward makes it all worthwhile.

> *Then your light shall break forth like the morning,*
> *Your healing shall spring forth speedily,*
> *And your righteousness shall go before you;*
> *The glory of the LORD shall be your rear guard.*
> *Then you shall call, and the LORD will answer;*
> *You shall cry, and He will say, 'Here I am'*
> *(Isaiah 58:8-9).*

Do you see it? The exceedingly abundantly above all we can ask or think manifests from within us! Our participation with God transforms us into the very image of the glory of the Lord (2 Corinthians 3:18). Jesus Christ—His very life—becomes our light, healing, and righteousness. The glory of the Lord is what we leave behind through the good works that glorify our Father in heaven (Matthew 5:16).

God is after a people who will embody His Son and walk in the good works He (the Father) has created (Ephesians 2:10). These are works He does Himself, for He receives the glory for them. We are simply the blessed instruments of an all-powerful God, and in the midst of this, He is responsive to our call and cry.

How could we resist so great a salvation as this?

Pray for me, and I will pray for you—that God would grant us grace and courage to pursue His opportunities.

Conclusion

> *And we know that all things work together for good to those who love God, to those who are the called according to His purpose (Romans 8:28).*

Romans 8:28 is one of the most encouraging verses in all of Scripture. It is also one of the most challenging to believe. Boy, what a difference one little word can make. "All things", not "some things", or just "things". God's attention span and orchestration defies imagination. He is an awesome God!

Furthermore, we have the promise that all things, no matter how tragic or whether we brought them on ourselves or not, work together for our good. How is that possible? How do we know such a thing?

The Greek word God chose to use for "know" in this verse literally means "to see". We will literally see all things work together for our good. Those who love God and have been called according to His purpose have been given eyes to see and ears to hear (Matthew 13:16). This is the promise to all who believe and follow the Lord, Jesus Christ.

Believe and follow Jesus into the storms and chaos, and you will discover God's purpose and orchestration *"to do exceedingly abundantly above all that we ask or think, according to the power that works in us. To Him be glory in the church by Christ Jesus to all generations, forever and ever. Amen"* (Ephesians 3:20-21).

CHAPTER 7

Participating in God's Restorative Work

Then Job answered the LORD and said:
"I know that You can do everything,
And that no purpose of Yours can be withheld from You."
Job 42:2

The LORD's purposes will not be withheld from Him.
Period. The storms and chaos of the 2020s will accomplish all He desires for the church. He will have the reign, intimacy, and habitation He envisioned before mankind's rebellion. The question we must give attention to is, "Will we and those we love benefit from the LORD's restorative work, or will we (and they) experience the great fall of our houses?"

Within the larger eternal context, God will accomplish exceedingly, abundantly more in our personal and corporate lives than we can think or imagine (Ephesians 3:20). How do we ensure the most positive outcome?

At this point, it is important to recognize that knowing the answer—even teaching the answer—is not the same as thinking about, believing, and acting on the answer. This is one of our carnal mind's most subtle and sinister deceptions. Subconsciously, it tells us, "I've got this," and we move on to a well-timed distraction. The appropriate response is, "No, I don't want you to have it. I want to discuss it with my

Creator, Lord, and Teacher. I want to know how They would have me respond."

We hope and pray you will find encouragement and direction in the following considerations.

Since learning about the eternal purposes of God some twenty years ago, I have searched out the matter and practiced the disciplines prescribed by God for participation in His restorative work. The questions you were challenged with in Chapter Three continue to challenge me.

- How complete is our surrender to the reign of Jesus Christ?
- How intimate is our prayer life?
- How invested are we in community with God's people?

Fortunately, our transformation is an iterative endeavor. God intends for us to diligently pursue maturity all the days of our lives. Only He knows the appropriate and most profitable pace.

The following includes several responses to God's purposes that have helped me along the way. As you consider them, listen carefully to the Holy Spirit. He will highlight one or two for your attention, and/or encourage you in something different.

Restoring Our Prayer Life

John Wesley has been quoted as saying, "God does nothing but in answer to prayer." While this may be a bit overstated (no one was here to pray creation into existence), when you consider the importance and magnitude of prayer, it is easy to understand the heart behind such a bold statement. Indeed, God does nothing in us and through us not channeled through prayer. Our spiritual strength, individually and corporately, is directly proportional to our attention to, investment in, and passion for relational prayer.

The importance of prayer in storms and chaos is so obvious, it seems a bit silly to even mention it. You would think, with the storms and chaos of this past year, church prayer meetings would be filled to capacity (regardless of the pandemic). Something has been tragically lost; we have become blind to the importance of prayer. So, with prayer and hope for the restoration of prayer in our individual and corporate lives, we offer the following helps and considerations. Each one has profoundly impacted my life and ministry.

Finding True Intimacy with God

The Father is working in us both to will and to do for His good pleasure (Philippians 2:13), which is to give us His kingdom (Luke 12:32). As bondservants, our hearts and minds turn to the will and desires of our Father in heaven. We discover God intends for our prayer life to be much more than we have settled for. He wants an intimate father-child relationship.

I have found the "PAPA Prayer" to be particularly helpful in this regard. Developed by Larry Crabb (2006), it follows an acrostic:

> **PRESENT** yourself to God: With authentic transparency, present whatever you discover in yourself—good or bad. Are you happy, sad, or mad? Disappointed or depressed? Be who you are, where you are. Humble children come as they are; and they trust their Father to receive them. Pretending can actually be a sign of pride.

ATTEND to how you are thinking of God: Focus on who God really is versus who you think God is, or who you want Him to be. Meditate on His names: El Elyon (Most High God), Adonai (Master), El Shaddai (God Almighty), 'El 'Olam (Eternal Creator).

PURGE yourself of anything that blocks your relationship with God: Eliminate whatever is blocking your intimacy with God by acknowledging, without excuse or explanation, the self-obsession the Spirit chooses to reveal. Begin by surrendering to His reign, followed by confession and repentance.

APPROACH God as the "first thing" in your life: Lay aside everything but God. Focus on Him as the only provider of truly good things. As you put Him first, you can then approach Him with the confidence that what He loves to give you is what you need the most.

Each step in the PAPA Prayer may expose a need for confession and repentance: for trying to hide your true feelings, for presuming Him to be something less than He is, for allowing things or people to come between you and God, or for making Him anything less than the first priority in your life. The conversation you have with Him in these areas will deepen and strengthen your relationship.

As Larry Crabb (2006) says, "Once you get a feel for it, praying relationally comes as naturally as breathing. Relating to God is what we were destined and designed to do."

Practicing the Presence of God

Our common ideas regarding prayer are not found in the New Testament. We look upon prayer simply as a means of getting things for ourselves, but the biblical purpose of prayer is that we may get to know God Himself. It is the only way we can get in touch with the truth and the reality of God Himself. To say that "prayer changes things" is not as close to the truth as saying, "Prayer changes me and then I change things." God has established things so that prayer, on the basis of redemption, changes the way a person looks at things. Prayer is not a matter of changing things externally, but one of working miracles in a person's inner nature (Chambers, 1992).

Prayer is difficult because our enemies do not want us communicating with God. Satan is a powerful being. An opposing power is needed—God's power. Is it possible our prayer life lacks God's power because we do not pray in the way God has designed? Have we chosen our own way in prayer?

Rejoice always, pray without ceasing, in everything give thanks; for this is the will of God in Christ Jesus for you (1 Thessalonians 5:16-18).

To "pray without ceasing" has also been called "practicing the presence of God". It is the blessing of a continual, conversational relationship with the One Who has all the answers. For most followers of Jesus, this seems like an unobtainable goal; but nothing could be further from the truth. The key to enjoying the continuous presence of God is relational prayer.

As we lay down our agenda—even our prayer list—and focus on Christ, a new dimension and opportunity for spiritual growth opens up to us.

But we all, with unveiled face, beholding as in a mirror the glory of the Lord, are being transformed into the same image from glory to glory, just as by the Spirit of the Lord (2 Corinthians 3:18).

As we behold the Lord's glory, the Holy Spirit works to renew our mind and open our mind's eye to see what we have been created and commanded to pursue.

But seek first the kingdom of God and His righteousness, and all these things shall be added to you (Matthew 6:33).

Jesus said it was the Father's good pleasure to give us the kingdom of God (Luke 12:32). We are to seek the very thing He intends to give. He is eager to give it.

Come to Me, all you who labor and are heavy laden, and I will give you rest. Take My yoke upon you and learn from Me, for I am gentle and lowly in heart, and you will find rest for your souls. For My yoke is easy and My burden is light (Matthew 11:28-30).

The relational approach to prayer is not a burden. If it seems so, then we must back up and ask God to expose why we are feeling and thinking this way. Most likely, we are still seeing Him as something He is not, or we are not praying out of a motivation to know Him.

Taking Every Thought Captive

It is quite common for potentially distracting thoughts to fight for our attention during prayer. Rather than immediately pushing these out of your mind, take them captive to the obedience of Christ.

> *For the weapons of our warfare are not carnal but mighty in God for pulling down strongholds, casting down arguments and every high thing that exalts itself against the knowledge of God, <u>bringing every thought into captivity to the obedience of Christ</u>, and being ready to punish all disobedience when your obedience is fulfilled (2 Corinthians 10:4-6).*

Ask the Lord what He would have you do with each of the thoughts you capture. He may tell you to put it aside. He may just as well tell you something He would like for you to do with it. For example, if it is about a meeting you have that day, He may want you to pray for the anticipated attendees. Or, the seemingly distracting thought may be an issue for which He wants to give you wisdom.

Whatever the case may be, our dedicated time of prayer is the perfect training ground for practicing His presence. As our conditioned response to distractions in prayer is transformed and we begin to turn to Him with them, it becomes easier to do the same when confronted with events and distractions during the day. Consequently, we are drawn further into the abiding life.

> *If you abide in Me, and My words abide in you, you will ask what you desire, and it shall be done for you (John 15:7).*

This verse highlights the relationship of the abiding life and the life of relational prayer. The prayer that discovers and accomplishes the desires of our hearts must begin in this abiding relationship. Our abiding in Him, and Him in us, is the relationship He desires.

Embracing Transformation

Our God is a process-oriented problem solver. He has a process (aka, a way) for every problem known to man. For those willing to search out the matter of God's problem-solving processes, there is glory in their discovery (Proverbs 25:2). Indeed, God's processes are found throughout Scripture, including His processes for salvation, sanctification, and faith.

Truly, God has a way for everything, including the restoration of our houses. Outside of God's prescribed way, chaos can be confusing and distracting, drawing us away from God's purposes in our lives. Chaos can become overwhelming and discouraging, threatening to destroy our destiny as kingdom citizens. On the other hand, within God's processes, chaos can be used by God to clarify and concentrate our focus, while empowering and encouraging us for kingdom assignments (i.e., the good works God created for us to walk in; Ephesians 2:10). God intends for chaos to draw us closer and transform us into the image of His Son's glory.

> But we all, with unveiled face, beholding as in a mirror the glory of the Lord, are being transformed into the same image from glory to glory, just as by the Spirit of the Lord (2 Corinthians 3:18).

Transformation is a unique process in that it occurs iteratively in the lives of every Christian who has submitted to the Holy Spirit's work. Through our beholding Christ's glory, the

Holy Spirit transforms us from one level of glory to the next; "out-raying" more of Christ's glory from one season of our lives to another.

Consider again the ugly, leaf-bound, leaf-eating caterpillar who *metamorphoos* into a beautiful, free-flying, nectar-eating butterfly (the Greek for transform is *metamorphoo)*. Dying to his old way and form, the caterpillar becomes a glorious new form of God's creation.

Similarly, God will use the chaos of this decade to dramatically transform the individuals, families, and fellowships who keep their eyes focused on the Lord and their minds set on things above. The Holy Spirit waits for God's people to submit to His transforming—*metamorphooing*—work. If they look carefully, every Christian who has been through the transformation process will recognize each of these seasons of transformation were bookended by a desire and an assignment.

The Desires of our Hearts

Man, consisting of both male and female, was created in the image of God (Genesis 1:26-27). One trait of this image is our purposefulness. "What is my purpose?" is one of the more revealing worldview questions, because it defines what we believe about ourselves and the world around us. Our Heavenly Father intends for us to know the purposes He has for us.

> To everything there is a season, a time for every purpose under heaven. (Ecclesiastes 3:1).

Every season in the life of every child of God has a purpose. Seasons come and seasons go (as they say) and, with them, the purposes of God for that season. If we miss it, the purpose

God has for us may be lost entirely, or it may be passed on to someone who will obediently respond. In some cases, God graciously and persistently offers a purpose to the same person multiple times.

How God orchestrates the many purposes He has for His many children is a mystery. But one thing we know, God reveals His purposes and does so through the desires of our hearts. As we mentioned earlier, the process of transformation begins with the discovery of these desires. The secret to the discovery of God's purpose for this season is found in the following verse:

> *Trust in the LORD, and do good; dwell in the land, and feed on His faithfulness. Delight yourself also in the LORD, and He shall give you the desires of your heart (Psalm 37:3-4).*

"He shall give you" is an emphatic promise of God. Of course, these are not our carnal desires, but those He intended before He established the foundations of the earth (Ephesians 2:10). God has been orchestrating events for thousands of years to help you discover the desires of your heart so He can give them to you.

Some fathers are blessed with the resources to plan ahead for a special gift they want to give their child, such as an education, a home, or the family business. But no father has been planning as long as your Heavenly Father for the desires He has put in your heart. So, how do we discover this special gift, and how do we position ourselves to receive it? By following the conditions of the promise:

1. Trust in the LORD: Take time to consider just how much you trust Him already. The exercise will build your faith in Him.
2. Do good: God opposes the wicked. We must lean into His goodness in word and deed.
3. Dwell in the land: The New Covenant land is God's kingdom, where dwelling is a matter of our relationship with Him as our King.
4. Feed on His faithfulness: Consider the testimonies of God's faithfulness in your life, the lives of people you know and have known, and those found in the Bible.
5. Delight yourself in Him: Trusting in His goodness and faithfulness, surrender to His reign.

Our God is a good god; our King, a good king! He desires and promises to give us the desires of our hearts. But there is a condition: we must delight in the LORD. Delight may not mean what you think it means. Here, and no other place in the Psalms, delight is translated from the Hebrew *anag*. *Anag* means "to be soft"—like clay in the Potter's hand (Isaiah 64:8).

In storms and chaos, we naturally attempt to take control of the situation or run away from it. Both represent the hard clay which the Potter finds impossible to mold and make for His purposes. Many times, the clay has been hardened by unbelief (Mark 16:14). Becoming soft again requires our waiting before the LORD as He applies and works in His living water, and works out the hard pieces of our unbelief. Being soft requires commitment and trust in the Potter.

Surrendering to the LORD's reign enables and empowers our faith during the storms. We learn trusting the Potter simply makes good sense. Laying down our ways of dealing with chaos to take on His become reasonable responses. After all, there is no other god like our God, who acts for the one who waits on Him (Isaiah 64:4).

> *Commit your way to the LORD,*
> *Trust also in Him,*
> *And He shall bring it to pass (Psalm 37:5).*

Keep in mind: the Potter loves the clay, even in its hardened state. He has desire, vision, and purpose for the clay—desires for good works, created and embedded in the heart of the clay before time (Ephesians 2:10). The Potter's good work in renewing the clay is a dramatic expression of His desire for intimacy. As we soften to His washing and working, we come to realize His heart's desire is our own—a heart tie between God and the object of His desire.

> *He shall bring forth your righteousness as the light,*
> *And your justice as the noonday (Psalm 37:6).*

The LORD's patient and persistent intimacy with His clay pays off in a big way for His glory AND the glory of the clay. Indeed, the finished product stretches our faith and imagination to their limits. And here we find the restoration of His habitation in mankind; here we discover the ultimate purpose of His reign and intimacy: He has made us become vessels of His glory through His Son, and this by the power of the Holy Spirit!

Surrendering to the LORD, we discover the desires of our heart are in His heart as well. That powerful and intimate connection with the heart of God will carry us through the trials and tribulations of transformation, and into the assignment He has prepared for us to walk in with Him. The desires of our hearts become the purposes of God, purposes that cannot be withheld from Him.

I know that You can do everything,
And that no purpose of Yours can be withheld from You
(Job 42:2).

Transformation

Early in my faith walk with Jesus, I heard preachers and teachers equate Christian maturity to other people "seeing more of Jesus in our lives". It sounded great, but I had no idea what they were talking about. How do I do that? What does that look like? I am sure someone must have encouraged me to ask myself, "What would Jesus do?" That just led to more questions: How should I know? Who else do I ask? What if I don't have time to hear, understand, and respond appropriately?

Eventually, I learned only Jesus could do what Jesus would do. I learned that for people to see more of Jesus, I had to get out of the way. As you might expect, that realization created a crisis of faith in my life. It was no longer okay to be a good and moral person, trusting that Jesus' death would get me into heaven. Standing at the cross is not the same as joining Jesus on it.

For whoever desires to save his life will lose it, but whoever loses his life for My sake and the gospel's will save it (Mark 8:35).

Determining to die so I might have life opened up heaven to me. Blessed with several disciple makers, I began to understand the mysteries of "in Christ" and the exchanged life (Galatians 2:20). This ultimately led to the discovery of 2 Corinthians 3:18 and *metamorphoo*, my favorite Greek word. The revelation astounded me and propelled my walk with the Lord. Finally, I understood the secret behind God's process for our maturation as Christians—that others might see more of Jesus in me.

> *Metamorphoo*: to change into another form, to transform, to transfigure; Christ's appearance was changed and was resplendent with divine brightness on the mount of transfiguration (*BlueLetterBible.com Outline of Biblical Usage*).

Our God, creator of the Greek language and the New Testament, chose to use *metamorphoo* in four strategic verses. A quick study of these reveals God's purpose and plan for allowing and creating storms and chaos in our lives. In addition to 2 Corinthians 3:18, we have:

> *Now after six days Jesus took Peter, James, and John his brother, led them up on a high mountain by themselves; and He was transfigured before them. His face shone like the sun, and His clothes became as white as the light (Matthew 17:1-2 [Mark 9:2-3 records the same event.]).*

It is no coincidence, and no small matter, that God uses *metamorphoo* to describe our transformation and Jesus' transfiguration. He could have chosen several other words, including "glorified". What exactly does this mean for us? To understand, we turn to a familiar passage:

> *Have this attitude in yourselves which was also in Christ Jesus, who, although He existed in the form of God, did not regard equality with God a thing to be grasped, but emptied Himself, taking the form of a bond-servant, and being made in the likeness of men (Philippians 2:5-7, NASV).*

Notice Jesus "emptied Himself" when He was made into the likeness of men. So, what did Peter, James, and John see when the Son of Man was transfigured? I believe they saw the glory of His Heavenly Father. He said as much to Phillip.

> *Jesus said to him, "Have I been so long with you, and yet you have not come to know Me, Philip? He who has seen Me has seen the Father; how can you say, 'Show us the Father'?" (John 14:9).*

What the disciples saw in Jesus every day, Peter, James, and John were blessed to see in its full manifestation on the Mount of *Metamorphoo*. They saw the glory of the Father. With that in mind, consider the same metaphysical relationship between the Father, His Son, and the remainder of God's children.

> *Let your light so shine before men, that they may see your good works and glorify your Father in heaven (Matthew 5:16).*

Notice the command here is not "do good works", but "let your light shine". What is that light?

> *In Him was life, and the life was the light of men (John 1:4).*

Jesus is the light we are commanded to let shine (not make shine; an important distinction). Consider further just who is glorified by the light men see in "your good works"? Would our just and loving Father take the glory of someone else's work, or the credit for their light? Of course not! Therefore, the good works must be His, as well as the light that is His life in Jesus. Jesus' prayer for those who would come after His disciples affirms this supernatural relationship.

And the glory which You gave Me I have given them, that they may be one just as We are one: *I in them, and You in Me;* that they may be made perfect in one, and that the world may know that You have sent Me, and have loved them as You have loved Me (John 17:22-23).

By coming to live in us, Jesus brings the glory of the Father with Him. As we are transformed, from glory to glory, people will see the good works created for us to walk in as the work of the Father. Now get this, the glory the Father gave to His Son, which His Son has given to us, will be returned to the Father. THAT is why we submit ourselves to the Holy Spirit's transformational power.

Finally, we come to the fourth and final occurrence of *metamorphoo.*

> *And do not be conformed to this world, but be transformed by the renewing of your mind, that you may prove what is that good and acceptable and perfect will of God (Romans 12:2).*

God will continue to use the storms and chaos of the 2020s to challenge our allegiances and expose our idols. We will be forced to choose between two radically different paths: conformity to the world or transformation by the renewing of our minds. Forcing the choice is the loving grace of our Father in heaven, who knows the dire consequences of our loitering around at the crossroads.

> *Then one said to Him, "Lord, are there few who are saved?" And He said to them, "Strive to enter through the narrow gate, for many, I say to you, will seek to enter and will not be able." (Luke 13:23-24).*

Many will not enter the kingdom for lack of striving. Others will miss incredible opportunities to experience God's glorious presence in their kingdom assignments.

Our Assignment

For we are His workmanship, created in Christ Jesus for good works, which God prepared beforehand that we should walk in them (Ephesians 2:10)

God orchestrates His problem-solving processes with great power and sovereign care. Indeed, He has been orchestrating each one of our individual lives and faith communities for this critical season. Even before the foundations of the world were laid, He prepared the good works we should walk in for His glory and the advance of His kingdom. We were created in Christ Jesus for our assigned participation in the good works of God. As challenging as the storms and chaos might be, the children of God can rest assured He will continue to orchestrate our passage through them (more on this in the next chapter).

The end of the transformation process comes when we are adequately prepared for the assignment that will glorify our Father in heaven. This assignment will be the physical manifestation of the desire of our heart. It is important to recognize and remember our preparation may be completed prior to the end of the chaos that prompted our transformation. Rather than wait for the storms to pass, we should begin looking for others to encourage and edify. This will likely be a substantial portion of our assignment. At some point, you will want to ask them about the desire of their heart.

Restoring Covenant

Work out your own salvation with fear and trembling; for it is God who works in you both to will and to do for His good pleasure (Philippians 2:12-13).

Understanding as we do, that the promises of God come to us by way of His covenants, and further understanding that covenants require the participation of two or more parties, it should interest us to know how we might participate with God in the establishment of His reign, intimacy, and habitation. Philippians 2:12-13 provides the general, overarching answer: we participate with God by working out our own salvation with fear and trembling.

Moreover, three critical truths found in this passage deserve our attention, particularly as we consider God's work in us to will and do for His good pleasure. First, our salvation must be worked out, suggesting it is not complete. Salvation is a process: we have been saved (Ephesians 2:8), we are being saved (1 Corinthians 1:18), and we shall be saved (Matthew 24:13). The implications of this cannot be overstated. The Christians most surprised by the fall of their houses will be those taught some twisted form of eternal security and/or perpetual prosperity.

Secondly, we discover God is working not only to "do", but to "will" for His good pleasure. Don't miss this: He takes responsibility for the willing and the doing, which begs the question: what responsibility has He left with us? As best as I have been able to understand, God leaves us with waiting on Him, hearing His voice, choosing His will, and trusting Him to accomplish the good work we find ourselves walking in. Easier said than done, but not as complicated and difficult as trying to will and do it ourselves.

Lastly, we should give serious consideration to the "fear and trembling" our participation with God requires. The primary meaning of fear (*phobos*) is dread and terror. Personally, I fear we have diminished the fear of the LORD to our spiritual harm. The judgment of God for those who do not endure to the end should concern us more than it does. Those who enter into heaven will themselves face the judgment seat of Christ. We would do well to consider the work required and its relationship to God's good pleasure. NOTE: We are not suggesting self-effort for our salvation, but participating with God as He works out His good pleasure.

In the context of storms, the initial step toward covenant with God is understanding His will for the chaos. In this regard, return to the Inspection Scorecard you completed in Chapter Three. First, with the Spirit's leading, select two or three areas in which you feel God would have you mature. Second, develop a plan with some immediate next steps (again with the Spirit's guidance). Only a few steps are needed to get you headed in the right direction.

Lastly, convert your plan into a written covenant with God. Don't skip this step. Our God is a covenant-keeping God. He will keep His promise to give you the desires of your heart; and He will lead you into the center of His will for this strategic season. You will learn surrender and submission to God's good work and fear of getting in His way. Ultimately, you will learn how to disciple others through God's way for their restoration.

Finding Hope in the Lukewarm Church

Is it possible the Church at Laodicea has been given an unfairly bad reputation? Sure, being rejected by the Lord is probably the worst thing that could happen to anyone. Being deceived about one's wretched, miserable, poor, blind, and naked condition is a sobering reminder of the Great Apostasy (2 Thessalonians 2:9-12). And it probably doesn't help that critical observation of the Western Church reminds us of Laodicea's lukewarm state.

Indeed, it is difficult to look beyond Jesus' rebuke and chastening of the Church at Laodicea. It is hard to get past the King's displeasure and the frightening consequences. Still, there is hope.

The Lord himself seems to have considerable hope for this much maligned church... and much to offer her. Let's take a look.

> *I counsel you to buy from Me gold refined in the fire, that you may be rich; and white garments, that you may be clothed, that the shame of your nakedness may not be revealed; and anoint your eyes with eye salve, that you may see. As many as I love, I rebuke and chasten. Therefore be zealous and repent. Behold, I stand at the door and knock. If anyone hears My voice and opens the door, I will come in to him and dine with him, and he with Me. To him who overcomes I will grant to sit with Me on My throne, as I also overcame and sat down with My Father on His throne (Revelation 3:18-21).*

It is truly amazing what the Lord offers the Church at Laodicea:

1. His kind and godly counsel;
2. To sell them what they need;
3. Loving rebuke and chastening;
4. Encouragement they are still capable of zealous repentance;

5. To dine with them; and,
6. A place with Him on His throne.

In short, our King offers restoration. How can we neglect so great a salvation, or so kind a king? What must we do to restore our relationship with Him? How do we turn this thing around?

1. Submit to His counsel;
2. Purchase and apply what He has offered;
3. Receive and respond to His rebuke and instruction;
4. Be zealous (burn with passion) and repent (change one's mind);
5. Hear His voice and open the door; and,
6. Overcome the deceptions and distractions in our lives.

The marvelous thing is that God the Father has already offered the grace we need for every one of these requirements. It is by grace, through faith, that we are saved (Ephesians 2:8-9). There is still hope for the lukewarm Church.

Perhaps this explains why God has sequestered us off from the world (or, if you prefer, the good He intends to work out of it). Could He be offering a reset and renewal? Could He be offering us encouragement for rest and repentance? Can you hear Him screaming?

He who has an ear, let him hear what the Spirit says to the churches (Revelation 3:22).

God bless you with grace for restoration—the exercise of ears you have been given, by the One who would see you overcome and enter into His kingdom. How can we neglect so great a salvation, or so kind a king?

Conclusion

Participating in God's restorative work requires humility, discipline, and a commitment to God's ways in all we do. God provides the grace and courage for everything He requires of us. His provision accomplishes our preparation for the storms. Our participation becomes a joyful adventure as we learn to navigate the chaos and lead others through it.

CHAPTER 8

Navigating the Chaos

And we know that all things work together for good to those who love God, to those who are the called according to His purpose. Romans 8:28

The normal Christian life—living as God truly intends—requires life investment and risk-taking. It includes tribulation, trial, persecution, and affliction. All these factors play a supernatural role in God's restorative work. We also know the Holy Spirit uses our sacrifice and suffering to transform us into the image of the glory of Christ (2 Corinthians 3:18). Truly, God works all things to the good of those who love Him and are called to His purpose. It should encourage us greatly to know our investment and suffering for God's kingdom has eternal value.

But what persuades us to go where so many fear to tread? And how do we persuade others to go with us? God has placed desires in our heart for every command and heavenly expectation, including desires to:

- Obey His call;
- Mature beyond the old status quo;
- Discover what is on the other side of our transformation;
- Walk with Him in the good works He has created specifically for us; and,
- Become strong houses of refuge, encouragement, and edification.

To prepare us for our future assignment, God allows, and even creates, chaos in our lives. Entering into the chaos willingly is a critical step in the restoration of our houses. Chaos tests us, helping us see what we truly believe. Chaos can be a great teacher, exposing our flesh and revealing the hard places of unbelief in our hearts. God uses chaos to search our hearts and shake loose the things that don't belong (Psalm 139:23-24). In this chapter, we will explore the ways God would have us navigate the chaos to His and our advantage.

There are several ways to respond to chaos. We can respond Satan's way, the world's way, man's way, or God's way. Satan's way is to lash out at those we think are causing the chaos, to manipulate others to get us out of it, or even throw innocent bystanders under the bus to feel better about our own discomfort. The world's way is to negotiate or ignore the chaos, so as to minimize its impact on our lives. Responding to chaos man's way usually includes our taking control of the situation, using whatever soulish skills we have to maneuver around it.

I have attempted many of the wrong ways for navigating through the chaos in my life. None have ended well. The times I have chosen to follow God's ways have been incredibly blessed.

Back in 2010, God taught my family some valuable lessons in chaos navigation through the trauma of a house fire and the chaos of finding another permanent residence. By God's grace, we followed Christ through one of the more incredible adventures of our lives.

As Beth and I watched our house go up in flames, the Lord said three things to me. The first was, "I am sovereign. Nothing happens outside of my will." He followed with, "I am a good God, I love you, and I have a plan for you. Reckon it so in your hearts." Lastly, the Lord said, "You will have to grieve." Those three words of encouragement were enough to get us started down the right path with God—a path of supernatural circumstance, extraordinary excitement, and unexpected blessing.

Our obedience to these commands—trust, reckon, and grieve—enabled us to walk confidently with the Lord in the adventure that would follow. Having previously emphasized the matter of trust in Chapter Six ("Restoring Our Faith in God's Faithfulness"), we will turn our attention to reckoning the truth and grieving the loss of old status quos.

To this point, our focus has been primarily one of "fixing what's broken"—restoring poorly laid foundations and shoddily built structures. It is hard to write about broken things without touching on the negative. Encouragement tends to take on a corrective tone. I truly wish it were not so, but it is what it is. That is why this chapter may turn out to be my (and your) favorite, for here we look to the fantastic grace of God, exploring the "exceedingly, abundantly more than we can ask or think"—those things He has prepared for every one of His children.

> *Most assuredly, I say to you, he who believes in Me, the works that I do he will do also; and greater works than these he will do, because I go to My Father (John 14:12).*

> *Now to Him who is able to do exceedingly abundantly above all that we ask or think, according to the power that works in us, to Him be glory in the church by Christ Jesus to all generations, forever and ever. Amen (Ephesians 3:20-21).*

These and many verses like them speak of the "greater works" God has made possible for His children. So, where are they? What must we do to walk in them? Is there a key that opens the door that leads to the life Jesus promised His followers?

One of the keys to the "greater-than" life is the renewing of our mind, particularly in regards to God's kingdom and our place in it. The renewal process plays a critical role in bridging the gap between hearing the word of God and walking in His good works—from the hearing of faith to the work of faith. We are transformed (*metamorphooed*) by the Holy Spirit through the renewing of our minds (Romans 12:2).

Our participation with the Holy Spirit begins and depends on our intentional and diligent reckoning of God's truth and reality. There is no more important time for this than in the storms and chaos of this life.

I must confess, my wife and I were a bit confused in the chaos of our house fire when God commanded us to reckon His goodness, love, and plan for our lives. What we were watching simply did not match what He was saying. As we discovered, that is why He told us to reckon it to be so: we needed our minds renewed for the adventure that would follow.

Being the Greek geek that I am, I eventually searched out the meaning of reckon. The search revealed a very simple but profound meaning. In secular Greek, *logizomai* is an accounting term, meaning "to pass to one's account"—something like an accountant balancing the books. Applied spiritually, reckoning is making true for oneself what God says is true—balancing my understanding of truth and reality with His. Indeed, one might argue it is laying hold of (or accessing) the mind of Christ.

Now, it is no small matter that *logizomai* appears in Scripture over forty times. Here are a few enlightening examples:

> *Likewise you also, **reckon** yourselves to be dead indeed to sin, but alive to God in Christ Jesus our Lord (Romans 6:11).*

> *For I **consider** that the sufferings of this present time are not worthy to be compared with the glory which shall be revealed in us (Romans 8:18).*

> *When I was a child, I spoke as a child, I **understood** as a child, I thought as a child; but when I became a man, I put away childish things (1 Corinthians 13:11).*

> *Finally, brethren, whatever things are true, whatever things are noble, whatever things are just, whatever things are pure, whatever things are lovely, whatever things are of good report, if there is any virtue and if there is anything praiseworthy—**meditate** on these things (Philippians 4:8).*

To understand the purpose and power of reckoning, let's take a walk through the process of faith and see how the great, empowering mysteries of God can be worked out in our lives. The process of faith consists of three steps:

1. The hearing of faith (Romans 10:17) – Hearing and believing a word from God.
2. Obedience to the faith (Romans 1:5; 16:26) – Determining to respond to God with appropriate action.
3. The work of faith (James 2:17-18) – Faith comes alive and is perfected through a physical response to God's word.

As with all kingdom processes, the process of faith begins with God. Before there is faith, there must be the hearing of the word of God.

So then faith comes by hearing, and hearing by the word of God (Romans 10:17).

The spoken word of God (*rhema*) produces the hearing of faith. God gives the ability to hear to those whose hearts have not grown cold (Matthew 13:11-17), that they might know the mysteries of the kingdom of heaven. Hearing is predicated on the condition of the heart to surrender to what God says (i.e., to believe and do His will).

For with the heart one believes unto righteousness, and with the mouth confession is made unto salvation (Romans 10:10).

Faith is a function of the heart. Therefore, we can say the word of God finds its resting place in the heart of the believer. The word of God and the faith it initiates lies in our heart waiting to come alive through and in the work God intends.

Do you see that faith was working together with his works, and by works faith was made perfect? For as the body without the spirit is dead, so faith without works is dead also (James 2:22, 26).

Without the accompanying work, the faith will die. Getting our faith to our feet, hands, and/or mouth is critically important. Dead faith is a stench in God's nostrils (like roadkill).

So, how does God's word and our faith find their way from heart to hands, feet, and mouth—the agents of God's good work? They must pass through our mind, which stands in the

middle of the faith process as a type of gatekeeper. To coop-
erate obediently, our mind must be renewed.

> *And do not be conformed to this world, but be trans-*
> *formed by the renewing of your mind, that you may prove*
> *[complete] what is that good and acceptable and perfect*
> *will of God (Romans 12:1-3).*

To prove or complete the will of God, we must first allow
God's will (i.e., what He has said) to renew our minds. This
is where reckoning comes in. In reckoning the word that has
been heard and believed, the mind is renewed by that word
and the measure of faith which comes with it.

> *But we all, with unveiled face, beholding as in a mirror*
> *the glory of the Lord, are being transformed into the same*
> *image from glory to glory, just as by the Spirit of the Lord*
> *(2 Corinthians 3:18).*

As we have learned previously, the renewing of our mind
transforms us into the very same image as the glory of the
Lord. We become more like the One who only does what
the Father is doing, in submission to His will. This begs the
question: how do we know the Father's will? We look inward,
where He is working for His good pleasure!

> *Therefore, my beloved, as you have always obeyed, not as*
> *in my presence only, but now much more in my absence,*
> *work out your own salvation with fear and trembling; for*
> *it is God who works in you both to will and to do for His*
> *good pleasure (Philippians 2:12-16).*

It is important to note the willing and the doing are God's
responsibilities. Rather than waste energy trying to do His good
work, we should focus our attention on the responsibilities

we have been given: making sure our hearts are surrendered, exercising the measure of faith we have been given, reckoning what He says to be true, and walking in the work He is doing. Reckoning is God's way for our participation with the Holy Spirit in the renewal of our minds for the work God the Father empowers.

If we will work out our salvation with fear and trembling, He will do His part to bring the supernatural life of Christ out of us; and we will be a blessing to Him and to the world around us. We will become strong houses of faith, experiencing the "greater than" life.

> *He who believes in Me, as the Scripture has said, out of his heart will flow rivers of living water (John 7:38).*

It should be noted: reckoning is not a positive-reinforcement technique. It is more than the power of positive thinking, because the power is not in our thinking, but rather in the thing we are thinking about: the word of God.

The "greater than" verses (e.g., John 14:12; Matthew 5:16; Ephesians 3:20) are an encouragement that what we hear from God is actually possible, through us and through those within our spheres of influence. The word of God becomes powerful when we reckon it to be so and we respond by walking in the work He has given us to accomplish for His kingdom. Reckoning becomes a spiritual, motivational, and physical force strong houses will use to encourage and edify others.

Let me go ahead and say it: the cost of the "greater than" life is high. Navigating the chaos requires steadfastness, strength of heart, and diligence. In consideration of the storms that lie ahead, it would be helpful to pause for a moment and reckon these truths for ourselves:

- Whatever the costs and whatever investments God requires, the return is far greater than any of us can imagine (2 Corinthians 4:17).
- More importantly, we must keep in mind that, though we benefit, we are not doing this for ourselves but for the One who loved us and gave His life for us (Galatians 2:20).
- Therefore, our investment is an opportunity to participate in His love for His Bride (Ephesians 5:25), and it is the privilege as His Wife to return that love to Him (Revelation 19:7). It is truly a double blessing.

Finally, righteousness is a gift we must reckon to be true in our lives, that we might be transformed from believing unto righteousness (Romans 10:10) to becoming the instruments of God's righteousness for those who seek refuge and encouragement in our strong houses.

> *And do not present your members as instruments of unrighteousness to sin, but present yourselves to God as being alive from the dead, and your members as instruments of righteousness to God (Romans 6:13).*

One of the more surprising lessons we learned during our house fire adventure relates to this matter of righteousness. We found God will use His children as His instrument of refuge and encouragement, even while they themselves are going through chaos. However, that would not have been possible if we had not obeyed God's command to grieve.

Grieving During Chaotic Times

The chaos we have experienced this year (2020) has been an incredible drag on personal and corporate productivity. How does one manage their time and the time of others in the midst of such uncertainty? How do we stay focused on God's purpose for our lives during the chaos?

As strange as it may sound, grieving offers a strategic advantage to the Christian who will go there and subsequently help their spheres of influence do the same. God is calling us to more—to a higher level of glory and kingdom productivity. To get there, we must grieve.

Chaos can be confusing and distracting, drawing us away from God's purpose in our lives. It can become overwhelming and discouraging, threatening to destroy our destiny as kingdom citizens. In other words, we become unproductive.

On the other hand, chaos can be used by God to clarify and concentrate our focus, while empowering and encouraging us for kingdom assignments—the good works God prepared for us to walk in (Ephesians 2:10). Furthermore, God intends for chaos to draw us closer to Himself and transform us into the image of His Son's glory.

Similarly, God will use the chaos of this decade to dramatically transform the individuals, families, and fellowships who keep their eyes focused on the Lord and their minds set on things above. The Holy Spirit waits for God's people to submit to His transforming—*metamorphooing*—work.

Like the caterpillar that must leave its old form to become a beautiful butterfly, our response to God's call requires leaving something behind. Many times, it is security, long held beliefs, routines, even people and places we have grown to love. Rarely does this call not involve dying to ourselves.

So, there must be grieving.

Grieving is not something most people readily embrace because we associate it with negative events. I am encouraging you to see grieving as the grace God has provided for all His children. Knowing our weaknesses, He has given us the process of grieving, that we might more easily and productively walk through the transformation required for our next assignment.

Here are at least four benefits of grieving:

1. Grieving prepares you to let go—making the first step possible. Saying goodbye is a liberating and empowering experience. Even when you don't know what you are leaving, offering up your "whatever" to God releases His grace for the journey.
2. Grieving allows you to keep your face turned in the right direction. God designed us to face toward the direction our feet are taking us, so we avoid tripping over obstacles and running into others. Spiritually speaking, those who keep looking back have a tough time finding God's path (and beholding the Lord).
3. Grieving makes future grieving easier, as God calls us to let go of more. Transformation is an iterative process. Dying to ourselves, that God might be our all-in-all is not a one-time event. As God proves Himself faithful in our letting go, we grow to trust Him for more.
4. Grieving liberates us from ourselves, that we might help others grieve (2 Corinthians 1:3-4). Those "others" are likely the people God has called us to run with, into the chaos and beyond.

Perhaps the most important thing I have learned about grieving is that it is a relational activity. God uses it to build our relationship with Him and others. Consequently, the beginning point for our grieving must be prayer. Both the PAPA Prayer

(Crabb, 2006) and the prayer of Psalm 139:23-24 are helpful tools in the grieving process.

> *Search me, O God, and know my heart;*
> *Try me, and know my anxieties;*
> *And see if there is any wicked way in me,*
> *And lead me in the way everlasting (Psalm 139:23-24).*

So, when you are ready to take the first step in your adventure toward the "greater-than" life, ask God to reveal something you need to leave behind—something that will allow you to practice the grieving process. He will meet you there with wisdom and grace to grieve your loss and help others to do the same.

God's Sanctifying Work in Chaos

Faithful stewards of the mysteries of God learn that revelation begets more revelation. One discovery of the truth broadens our mindset to reveal or further explain the topography and ways of God's kingdom. It's like a steward finding fertile ground on the backside of his master's estate, seeking to make the most of it, and then plowing up large nuggets of gold. For some reason, I have in my mind's eye Jed Clampett shooting at a rabbit and discovering oil.

Anyway, back to the reality of our Father's kingdom...

> *So I say to you, ask, and it will be given to you; seek, and you will find; knock, and it will be opened to you (Luke 11:9).*

> *Blessed are those who hunger and thirst for righteousness, For they shall be filled (Matthew 5:6).*

God is not hiding the truth from us, that we might never find it. He lovingly accommodates those with an expressed interest in faithful stewardship.

> It is the glory of God to conceal a matter,
> But the glory of kings is to search out a matter (Proverbs 25:2).

This matter of grieving encourages us to further search out some of the most challenging and unavoidable questions in Christendom:

- Why would God allow or cause His children to suffer?
- How does our suffering line up with God working all things to our good?
- How do we encourage ourselves and others in the midst of suffering?

The fact Satan, the world, and our carnal mind use these questions in their attempts to undermine our faith does not make them bad questions. On the contrary, a faithful searching will encourage us further in God's loving purposes for the chaos He has called us and others to navigate. Navigating through the chaos with an understanding of God's sanctifying work will greatly help us maximize the suffering chaos inevitably creates. What our enemies intend for evil, God will turn to our good.

Sanctification—being set apart for God's use—is a major theme of Scripture and a blessed outcome of God's work in storms and chaos, if we allow it (James 1:2-4). Participating with God in our sanctification requires a reasonable level of understanding. We must recognize God would have us separate ourselves from both the world and our flesh. Like barnacles and rebellious sailors, the world and our flesh must be scraped away and cast overboard if we are to successfully navigate chaotic waters.

The Good Purpose of Suffering

God uses all forms of suffering to separate our newly created spiritual self from our flesh and the world. In a very real sense, our new, born-of-God self is not negatively affected by persecution, affliction, trial, and tribulation (unless we allow it). On the contrary, a proper perspective will produce blessed rejoicing and leaps of joy!

> *Blessed are you when men hate you,*
> *And when they exclude you,*
> *And revile you, and cast out your name as evil,*
> *For the Son of Man's sake.*
> *Rejoice in that day and leap for joy!*
> *For indeed your reward is great in heaven,*
> *For in like manner their fathers did to the prophets*
> *(Luke 6:22-23).*

Handled correctly, suffering mortifies the flesh and exposes the carnal mind's pitiful self-centeredness, while turning and drawing the new man to God and His kingdom. When we love God and our enemies, God enters into our suffering with power and protection from the whining influence of our flesh. With our flesh and carnal mind effectively silenced, hearing and obeying God's voice becomes a more regular response to suffering.

Furthermore, the sufferings of this world remind us there are two kingdoms. Our flesh resides in the lower realm of darkness while we—the ones born of God—enjoy the upper kingdom of light. Consequently, our separation from our flesh and its mind is worked out supernaturally when we deny ourselves, take up our cross, and follow Jesus into His life of sacrificial love for brothers, neighbors, and enemies. In other words, embracing the suffering God allows into our lives helps drive a wedge between our spirit man and our flesh.

As born-again children of God, we must be very careful to avoid settling for the compromised condition where our flesh does not complain too much and we do not feel too awkwardly separated from God. This is a gray and lukewarm place, and a deception of our carnal mind and Satan. It is a place of hand-holding and conspiracy with the enemies of God (James 4:4-5).

As those born of God, we must force ourselves to see the contrast of light and darkness from a heavenly perspective, suspiciously inspect our subconscious thinking, courageously categorize everything into these two extremes, and earnestly strive to enter through the narrow gate, down the difficult path that leads to life (Matthew 7:14).

Using Chaos as a Wedge

Similarly, the chaos we will continue to face through much of the 2020s is intended by God to drive a wedge between our spirit man and the world. The individuals, families, and fellowships who choose God's way through the chaos will enjoy His grace and glory. Sadly, others will allow the chaos to further conform them to the world and its ways (Romans 12:2).

So, how do we join God in the process and help others do the same? The answer can be found in a few familiar passages.

Trust in the LORD, and do good;
Dwell in the land, and feed on His faithfulness.

129

Delight yourself also in the LORD,
And He shall give you the desires of your heart (Psalm
37:3-4).

Separation from our flesh and the world begins with trust in the LORD—for His grace and faithfulness in the process (Step 1). It will help to know "the land" is His kingdom, and "delight" means to be soft (i.e., surrendered to His molding hands). The LORD owns the process and knows best how to apply it to His people.

Furthermore, the LORD puts His desire for separation into our hearts. These heart ties draw us into His presence and love, and sustain us when separation from our flesh and the world becomes difficult and painful. The Holy Spirit patiently waits for us to invite Him to stir up the desire of our heart for separation unto the LORD (Step 2).

I beseech you therefore, brethren, by the mercies of God,
that you present your bodies a living sacrifice, holy, accept-
able to God, which is your reasonable service (Romans
12:1).

Encouraged and motivated by our heart tie with God, we come to offer our entire being for His use (Step 3). This offering does not include our carnal flesh, but only that which is holy (i.e., our spirit man). That does not mean the sacrifice will be without pain. The consuming fire of God will further purity us for His use. We must be willing and prepared for the required chaos and suffering (Step 4). We must set our mind on things above and serve from a heavenly perspective (Step 5).

Romans 12:2 reminds us the world and our carnal mind must be actively and aggressively resisted (Step 6). Victory comes *"by grace ... through faith, and that not of yourselves; it is the gift of God..."* (Ephesians 2:8). However, we are responsible for hearing and obedience to the faith of God's word (Romans 10:17; 16:26).

Our flesh and the world offer innumerable carnal means and methods for navigating the chaos we will face in the 2020s— all compromising deceptions (i.e., veils) that separate us from God. For those born of God, there is only one Way, Truth, and Life. He is our Lord, Jesus Christ. Our liberty is found only in Him, His Spirit, and the grace of His Father. We must reject carnal means and methods (Step 7).

Our heads have been placed on our bodies facing the direction we most often move to generally keep us from hurting ourselves. Navigating the chaos requires our full attention. We must avoid looking back at the flesh and world left in our wake; if necessary (and it often is), let us grieve and get on with it (Step 8). Additionally, the current and ongoing distractions of our whiny flesh and the hedonistic world must be ignored (think spiritual blinders; Step 9).

Thankfully, we have only to look upon the One who has won our hearts (Step 10). His glory is captivating to all who will become His wife. Beholding His glory, we are transformed by the Holy Spirit and separated from the world.

> Turn your eyes upon Jesus
> Look full in His wonderful face
> And the things of Earth will grow strangely dim
> In the light of His glory and grace
> (Helen Howarth Lemmel).

2020 has been a time of preparation for the Church of our Lord, Jesus Christ. God's desire has been the separation of our spirit man from our flesh and the world. Those who continue to resist will find themselves further bound and conformed. There is still some amount of time—who knows how little—to begin allowing the chaos and suffering to do God's work. But we best get on with it.

Again, this applies to both individuals and groups of all sizes. In fact, facing chaos and suffering alone is both perilous and unnecessary. Wars are best fought in platoons; there are no Lone Rangers in the body of Christ. So, find (or form) a small fellowship who will commit to God's desires for the chaos. The sooner, the better; in fact, go ahead and move this to the beginning of the process (Step 0).

Lessons While Cycling—Staying Focused on the Climbs

I ride my bicycle to commune with God; the exercise is icing on the cake. Our conversations are most often about people He has me praying for, conversations I need to have with others, or lessons we are preparing to write or teach. Every once in a while, God uses the ride to show me something about myself and/or His kingdom.

Distractions are a big part of cycling—passing cars and approaching dogs in particular. Most are not a threat, but it only takes one. Having to deal with them on a regular basis has taught me to allow distraction when necessary, and then get back to the matter at hand. It has become a natural part of the process.

I wish I could say the same about hills.

Hills are different from cars and dogs. They don't generate the same adrenaline spike as a ferocious dog on the loose or a driver passing at a curve. In fact, they don't scare me at all. On the other hand, they last longer, the distress builds over time, and the distraction is my own discomfort and pain.

Hills are a major distraction to my communion with God.

For me, hills are a metaphor for the challenging seasons of our lives. These may be momentary, lengthy, or any amount of time in between. God has used the hills in my life to reveal a few things about myself and my relationship with Him:

1. The more I focus on the pain, the greater the pain becomes.
2. When I set my mind on things above, the hill is not only less of a distraction, but easier to navigate.
3. The approach I take has a dramatically positive effect on my mental and physical response to the effort after cresting the hill.
4. It occurs to me as I write this that having a riding partner to remind me of these things—and encourage me in them during the climb—would be an incredible blessing.

Setting my mind on things above is the key. Most often that involves praise and thanksgiving, and prayer for others. I am particularly fond of the Doxology, the Lord's Prayer, and praying the Apostolic Prayers for others.

In case you are wondering, this is all done in my head; gasping for air is about all I can do with my mouth and lungs.

Admittedly, applying this to the challenging seasons of our lives is more difficult. It requires more awareness and sensitivity to other elements of our being (e.g., our emotions). On the other hand, it is easier to open your Bible, tune in a praise song on the radio, or call a brother or sister in Christ, when you're not sitting on a bicycle.

Whether you're slugging it up a hill on a bicycle, or navigating through a challenging season of life, God has a very personal way for you to stay connected with Him. Search out the matter with Him. He loves talking with His children. Set your mind on things above; He will help you keep it there.

More Lessons from Our House Fire Adventure

God was truly gracious to us as we walked through the storm and chaos created by the destruction of our home. He responded to our trust, reckoning, and grieving with many other lessons. I trust God will use them to help you—and help you to help others—through the chaos most of us are already experiencing. Meditate on the referenced verses, allowing them to renew your mind.

1. Intentionally recognize the sovereignty of God and the truth of Romans 8:28.
2. Praise Him for His faithfulness; He inhabits the praises of His people (1 Peter 4:19).
3. Stay focused on Him; distractions are your enemies (Luke 9:62).
4. Stay in the now, recognizing the chaos is as much about your transformation as it is about your future (2 Corinthians 3:18).
5. Daily choose to surrender, sacrifice and submit for His glory (Luke 9:23).
6. Exercise your faith by challenging yourself with His promises. Psalms 34 and 37 are good places to start. If you believe these promises, then speak them to yourself out loud. If you do not believe them, ask God to

give you the faith you need. He uses chaos to increase our faith.

7. Pursue a deeper relationship with the Lord by practicing the PAPA prayer. There is no more important time to protect your intimacy with the Lord than when you are in chaos (Hebrews 4:16).

8. Draw your strength and encouragement from the Lord. Aggressively resist all sources of assistance which are not clearly from Him (Ephesians 6:10).

9. Go with others, leaning on your church fellowship and your close Christian friends. Add to these at least three others you can trust to pray for your protection and transformation (Ephesians 6:18-19).

Following these nine steps will not only help you survive the chaos; it will ensure you maximize God's purpose and plan for it. It will turn what would otherwise be an utterly miserable experience to one of exciting adventure. It will encourage, edify, and equip you for joyful, Spirit-filled ministry.[2]

Concluding Encouragement to Leaders

First, I want you to know I have been praying for you—some specifically, and all of you generally, as strategically positioned children of God and instruments of His grace. Second, I want to offer you some encouragement. Please take the following to God in prayer, asking Him to speak into your situation.

God gives insight, wisdom, and revelation to His people during times of crisis. He provides supernatural solutions to the problems a crisis creates (problems are His opportunities). This is one of the ways He works all things to the good of those

---

[2] The full account of our house fire adventure has been included in the appendix as a testimony to God's faithfulness, power, and love.

who love Him and are called to His purpose. They are opportunities to turn what Satan meant for evil into good. God uses people like you, in circumstances like this, to glorify Himself through the good work He has created for you to walk in.

With all this in mind, there are some strategic questions you can take to God.

1. What problem has this crisis created that God would use you to solve for His glory?
2. How might you repurpose what may be going away or contracting (e.g., the office furniture business into home office consulting and supply)?
3. Who are the future partners God has placed in your sphere? Do not dismiss a seemingly unrelated connection; God's solutions are often beyond our imagination.
4. How do we maintain (even build) community within the company? How does this apply to current and potential customers?
5. How can I use this time to help my current and potential clients (e.g., create a guide for remote work management and support)?

Remember: A part of God's image created into the image of mankind is creativity. Also, you have been given ears to hear, so you might understand the mysteries of His kingdom. The Father loves talking with His children—particularly those who will listen. Whatever you do, please do not waste this opportunity to commune with God. He is trying to get our attention for one reason or another. Perhaps the best first question is, "God, what do you want to talk about?"

Finally, it is always important during times like this to check in with your heart and see what desires God may be stirring there. He has promised to give them to you (Psalm 37:4). God bless you with courage and grace for the insight, wisdom, and revelation you receive from Him.

Conclusion

For those bound for more glory, there is no getting around the chaos. It is part of the normal Christian life. So, let's not waste the pain. Take full advantage by knowing and accepting the ways of God in the chaos that accompanies the transformation process.

Furthermore, no one should face trials and tribulations alone. Chaos is best met within communities where we can trust others to watch our back and encourage us to keep moving forward. God has encouraged and equipped you to be His agent of encouragement and guidance. Without a shepherd, the sheep will be scattered. Many will become discouraged and will be destroyed without your help.

A Pause for Renewed Consideration

Pausing to consider the LORD's objective for this book and the distance we have traveled to this point, one might become overwhelmed in the breadth and depth of God's purposes for their house. Perhaps this is His intention. After all, He is a big god with big plans. Therefore, we must remind ourselves: becoming a house who will stand in the storms and chaos of the 2020s will not be as hard as we think—particularly when we think from God's perspective.

Most of us have weathered a storm or two with natural grit, personal determination, and human reason. And we remember, it was hard work. Additionally, many seem to have an innate ability to navigate around chaos; others have the means—psychologically and/or physically—to isolate themselves from a storm's impact. Regrettably, when it comes to our spiritual house, avoidance strategies inevitably lead to disaster. For Christians in particular, the coming storms and chaos will be devastating for those who attempt to endure or avoid them naturally.

Ironically, we (yes, even Christians) tend to admire individuals who come through storms and chaos unscathed and unaffected. The irony of this will only make sense to kingdom citizens, for only in the kingdom do weaknesses lead to strength.

Therefore I take pleasure in infirmities, in reproaches, in needs, in persecutions, in distresses, for Christ's sake. For when I am weak, then I am strong (2 Corinthians 12:10).

Someone reading this interlude will benefit from considering God's desires and purposes in making our houses strong enough to withstand the coming storms and chaos. He is working in us to will and to do for His good pleasure and for His name's sake (Ezekiel 36:22). Furthermore, like Job, we are uplifted and invigorated in the confidence that God can do everything, and no purpose of His can be withheld from Him (Job 42:2).

As we turn the corner toward spiritually abiding in our restored house, be encouraged that the Father, Son, and Holy Spirit have committed Themselves to diligently work in you for Their purposes in your life. Your hearing to this point has deposited a fresh measure of faith into your heart (Romans 10:17). That faith will be released to lay hold of every bit of grace you need to glorify our Father in heaven, as you choose to become a strong house of refuge, encouragement, and edification for those who have lost theirs.

At this point, you may hear a voice from somewhere inside your head say, "But I am not ready for this!" Don't let that thought discourage or distract you. Remember, God can do exceedingly abundantly more than we can ask or think (Ephesians 3:20). He can do all He intends with very little human resource. Truly, your *here* (in space) and your *now* (in time) are well within His providence.

Choosing to do God's will appropriates and activates the grace and wisdom of God each one of us requires. The greatest kingdom adventures begin with the slightest indication of our willingness. Choosing leans us into the warm and loving heart of God, where we find our own refuge, encouragement, and edification—more than enough for ourselves and others.

Step Three – Abide

CHAPTER 9

Abiding in Christ

Metaphors are created to stretch earthbound paradigms and, in our case, to introduce kingdom principles. However, natural metaphors, by their nature, eventually disappoint—particularly when employed to describe the supernatural. For example, how does one abide in the house who is metaphorically themself? Fortunately, all is not lost; the supernatural realm comes to the rescue.

Though it may fail technically, the metaphor of "abiding" serves its purpose well, for it introduces one of the greatest metaphorical revelations known to man: our abiding in Christ. Indeed, we find the principle of abiding closer to the truth for our house than we might first anticipate, for "abiding" ensures the strength and security of our house, as well as its usefulness as a refuge of encouragement, edification, and service to others.

The Meaning of Abide

Abide (menō): To remain; in reference to place, to sojourn, tarry, not to depart; in reference to time, to continue to be, not to perish, to last, endure; in reference to state or condition, to remain as one, not to become another or different; to wait for, await one *(BlueLetterBible.com Outline of Biblical Usage).*

The New Testament begins with houses who stand (or fall) in the storm, introduces a spiritual house built of living stones—that's us (1 Peter 2:4-5), and culminates with a city, coming down from heaven, prepared as a bride adorned for her husband (Revelation 21:2), to serve as the abode of God (v. 3). This eternal city is God's creation and yet, "His wife <u>has made herself</u> ready (Revelation 19:7)." How does this happen? How do we get from here to there?

We abide in Christ.

Abiding in Christ catalyzes and sustains our preparation for His abiding in us. As we abide in Jesus, He, His Father, and the Holy Spirit abide in us, both individually and corporately (1 John 4:12-16). Such an encouraging and inspiring mystery can only be understood through experience—like knowing the feeling of "wet". Only willful and diligent participation in the biblical promises and conditions of God will get us there.

Notice also that "abide" extends beyond place and time to a person's state of being. It also includes anticipation—"to wait for, await one". Truly, "abide" contains a depth of meaning beyond the capability of our natural minds. As we will discover, it is one of God's most important mysteries.

The Importance of Abiding

> *I am the vine, you are the branches. He who abides in Me, and I in him, bears much fruit; for without Me you can do nothing. If anyone does not abide in Me, he is cast out as a branch and is withered; and they gather them and throw them into the fire, and they are burned. If you abide in Me, and My words abide in you, you will ask what you desire, and it shall be done for you. By this My*

Father is glorified, that you bear much fruit; so you will be My disciples (John 15:5-8).

Every Christian should be familiar with this passage. From it, we know the life of the vine flows through the branches to produce its fruit. Branches don't produce fruit. They transport the life that produces the fruit. They are blessed in this limited but important function. At least four very important things are promised to those who abide in Christ:

First: "He... bears much fruit... without me you can do nothing." – We are promised to be neither barren nor unfruitful. Our fruitfulness in God's kingdom is dependent on and directly related to our abiding in His Son. There is no other way to be productive in God's kingdom. Christ said the same thing about Himself (John 5:19). He then sent His disciples in the same way His Father sent Him (John 20:21). It is the abiding life of Christ that does what He did.

Second: "...you will ask what you desire, and it shall be done for you." – The meaning of this verse goes back to Psalm 37:4. It is the will of God to give us the desires of our hearts. As we abide in Christ, we discover those desires, ask for them, and they immediately become the purposes of God that will not be denied Him (Job 42:2).

Third: "My Father is glorified, that you bear much fruit..." – This is the physical manifestation of the power of abiding. The fruit that glorifies the Father are the greater-than works of John 14:12; even works greater than those He did through Jesus. These are the good works of Matthew 5:16—works that others will look at and say, "Isn't God awesome!" As we abide in Christ, God's supernatural work becomes the fruit of our life. This is the life for which we were created: to glorify our Father in heaven.

Lastly: "...you will be My disciples." – This abiding, fruit producing, Father glorifying life is the requirement of every disciple of Christ. A sobering thought: those who are not abiding are not producing, they are not glorifying the Father, and they are not His. Therefore, we must discover how to abide, and how to disciple others into an abiding relationship with Christ.

Keys to Abiding

Now that we understand the gravity of abiding in Christ, let's continue searching to find the keys we need to partake of His life.

> *But you do not have His word abiding in you, because whom He sent, Him you do not believe (John 5:38).*

The word of God did not abide in the Jewish leaders because they did not believe Jesus was the Christ. Abiding requires believing in Christ. It comes by faith, not by mental exercise. Faith comes by hearing and hearing by the word of God (Romans 10:17), and it is with the heart that man believes (Romans 10:10).

It is not surprising that our belief in Jesus is the beginning of the abiding life; and that there is more.

> *Therefore let that abide in you which you heard from the beginning. If what you heard from the beginning abides in you, you also will abide in the Son and in the Father (1 John 2:24-25).*

All we have heard from God contributes to our abiding in the Son and the Father: through the teaching, preaching, and reading of God's word; through reading Christian literature;

and, through the direct words that come from God in prayer, meditation, dreams, godly counsel, etc. This is great news!

However, we must remember that anyone who is *"a hearer of the word and not a doer, is like a man observing his natural face in a mirror; for he observes himself, goes away, and immediately forgets what kind of man he was"* (James 1:23). His faith dies for lack of the accompanying and perfecting work (James 2:22).

The abiding life requires more than hearing and believing. We must obey what we hear.

> *But whoever keeps His word, truly the love of God is perfected in him. By this we know that we are in Him. He who says he abides in Him ought himself also to walk just as He walked (1 John 2:5-6).*

We must walk as Christ walked—in perfect obedience to the Father.

> *As the Father loved Me, I also have loved you; abide in My love. If you keep My commandments, you will abide in My love, just as I have kept My Father's commandments and abide in His love (John 15:9-10).*

As Jesus kept His Father's commandments and abides in His love, we must do the same in Jesus. By keeping His commandments, we will abide in His love, and the love of God will be perfected in us. In this we can be confident we abide in Him.

As you can see, our part in abiding is not complicated: hear, believe, and obey. It is a blessing to know our loving Father has made it simple enough for children to understand. The faith of a child, with a heart to respond, is all that is required for us to find the power of abiding.

As we submit to the abiding life, the Father draws us deeper into the mystery. He reveals more of His kingdom, we hear more clearly, and our faith grows. As we respond in obedience, our abiding is strengthened and the cycle of increased maturity continues, from faith to faith and glory to glory.

The Sacrament of Holy Communion

There is another way—a particularly supernatural way—we come to abide in Jesus Christ: through the sacrament of Holy Communion. As with all the sacraments, communion is a sacred moment—a moment in God's presence when we have the opportunity for God to do something supernatural in each of us and in the corporate body to which we belong.

Very early in His ministry, Jesus had some profound things to say about communion. Here are a few excerpts from the sixth chapter of John's Gospel:

> *Do not labor for the food which perishes, but for the food which endures to everlasting life, which the Son of Man will give you, because God the Father has set His seal on Him (v. 27).*

Jesus is encouraging them to think beyond what they have seen—the feeding of the five thousand.

> *Then they said to Him, "What shall we do, that we may work the works of God?" (v. 28).*

Still, their minds are stuck on the miracle—the physical evidence of His power. Without chastening (because the works are important), Jesus encourages them again to think beyond that which can be seen.

> *Jesus answered and said to them, "This is the work of God, that you believe in Him whom He sent." (v. 29).*

Interestingly, here we see again the first step of abiding: belief in Jesus. But their confusion continues, and they ask Him for a greater sign, something like the manna given in the desert (vv. 30-31). In response, He makes this profound statement:

> *For the bread of God is He who comes down from heaven and gives life to the world. Then they said to Him, "Lord, give us this bread always." And Jesus said to them, "I am the bread of life. He who comes to Me shall never hunger, and he who believes in Me shall never thirst." (vv. 33-35).*

The mystery deepens as Jesus reveals He will not only give them "the food which endures to everlasting life" (v. 27), but He is that food. With passion, He encourages them to come and believe. Then, He pushes them beyond their comfort zone:

> *Most assuredly, I say to you, unless you eat the flesh of the Son of Man and drink His blood, you have no life in you. Whoever eats My flesh and drinks My blood has eternal life, and I will raise him up at the last day. For My flesh is food indeed, and My blood is drink indeed. He who eats My flesh and drinks My blood abides in Me, and I in him (vv. 53-56).*

This is critically important: rather than reject this word of Jesus (as so many did), or pass over it because we cannot grasp its meaning with our natural minds, let's pause to let the Holy

Spirit speak. Just to be clear, I am suggesting a pause to ask the Holy Spirit for revelation into this mystery. Put the book down, and come back later if necessary. Don't miss this great opportunity to hear what the Spirit is saying to the churches.

Now, while recognizing the limitations of mind and pen and acknowledging there is mystery here which I cannot put into words, let me share what these verses mean to me:

The supernatural work of God through communion is Him further abiding us in Jesus Christ and each other. When a follower of Jesus takes communion in faith and reverence, God strengthens their abiding in His Son and His Body.

This explains the importance of approaching communion in reverence and faith. To come any other way is to waste the sacred moment of communion. Paul put it this way:

Therefore, my beloved, as you have always obeyed, not as in my presence only, but now much more in my absence, work out your own salvation with fear and trembling; for it is God who works in you both to will and to do for His good pleasure (Philippians 2:12-13).

In response to our working out our salvation with fear and trembling, God works in us for His good pleasure—abiding us in His Son; and thereby giving us His kingdom (Luke 12:32).

Furthermore, in strengthening our abiding in Christ, the Father also strengthens our fellowship with each other. This is why we take communion with the community of believers. Our communion is with Jesus and with the Jesus in each other. In communion, the power of abiding is also the power of community.

Abiding in Christ is one of the greatest mysteries of the kingdom; and one of the most powerful. Not only does abiding release the power of God in our lives, but it marks us as a disciple of Christ. If we abide, we will be fruitful—and assured of an abundant entrance into the kingdom of God.

Conclusion

Abiding in Christ is one of the greatest mysteries of the kingdom; and one of the most powerful. That God would institute a sacrament for this purpose speaks powerfully to His desire for us to abide in His Son. Not only does abiding release the power of God in our lives, but it marks us as a disciple of Christ. If we abide, we will be fruitful—and assured of an abundant entrance into the kingdom of God.

Furthermore, abiding in Christ is the obvious next step in God's plan for our eternally secure and ever-strengthening house. Without the life of Christ, our efforts to protect and maintain our house (the next chapter) will become frustrating and discouraging, and our service to others (the last chapter of this section) will be powerless and fruitless

CHAPTER 10

Protection and Maintenance

For in it the righteousness of God is revealed from faith to faith; as it is written, "The just shall live by faith."
Romans 1:17

S piritual maturity is an ongoing process. If we will allow Them, the Father, Son, and Holy Spirit will continue to expand our footprint and our influence on this side of heaven. This is, of course, a primary reason we have endured inspection and restoration: that our growth will be on solid foundation, to support the good work God has created for us to walk in (Ephesians 2:10).

Were it not for God's enemies, the way from here would be easy. But the restoration of our houses has not gone unnoticed. Satan's deceptions have been exposed, exhumed, and tossed out. He has noticed and is understandably furious.

Similarly, the world has noticed our rejection of its temporal designs and building methods, and we have likely disturbed once comfortable relationships. Last but not least, our flesh and its carnal mind have been exposed as enemies in the camp. Though turned back, each of our enemies will desperately hang on to as much influence as they can; counter-attacks are to be expected.

Physical houses must be protected from invaders: bug barriers must be maintained, exterior surfaces regularly painted, and roofs eventually replaced. Leave a house long enough and you will return to find trees growing up through floorboards and vines insidiously covering the entire structure. Left unattended, our spiritual houses will creep into the same disrepair. Homeowners have a responsibility to protect their homes (just ask your Homeowners Association).

A healthy house must also be maintained: floors vacuumed, tubs and toilets cleaned, air filters replaced, and don't get me started on the yardwork. Home maintenance is a never-ending endeavor. By the way, I am not complaining. It is a blessing and privilege to be entrusted with a house, and a joy to turn it into a home. The same can be said for our spiritual house.

God has given us several ways to protect and maintain our house in the midst of storms and chaos. What the enemy intends for evil, God will turn to good... if we will follow His ways.

The Ways of God

*And now, Israel, what does the LORD your God require of you, but to fear the LORD your God, to **walk in all His ways** and to love Him, to serve the LORD your God with all your heart and with all your soul, and to keep the commandments of the LORD and His statutes which I command you today **for your good** (Deuteronomy 10:12-13).*

The LORD our God requires that we walk in all His ways, for our good and His glory. Failing to follow God's ways is a sure way to compromise the integrity of our house. Our enemies are constantly offering counterfeit ways and distractions. Consequently, commitment to the ways of God is mission critical to protecting and maintaining a house who will stand in the storms.

> *Commit your way to the Lord,*
> *Trust also in Him,*
> *And He shall bring it to pass (Psalm 37:5).*

God is a process-oriented problem solver (I never tire of saying or writing that). He has a process for every problem known to mankind, and every problem man has introduced into His kingdom. God has a way for everything. Some of His ways are clearly laid out in Scripture, others come to us as wisdom or in-the-moment direction from the Holy Spirit.

Observing the ways of God requires understanding and practice. For example, the way of God for our transformation requires our active participation with the Holy Spirit in the renewal of our minds. God's ways are too numerous for us to reference in their entirety here. However, several are particularly important to the protection and maintenance of our house, and our abiding therein. Please consider the following as a starting point and encouragement for further searching out the ways of God (Proverbs 25:2).

The Process of Salvation

How ironic that we give so much attention to events, when life is such an amazing process. Why are we so enamored with milestones? Perhaps we subconsciously avoid investing the mental energy required to keep the process in mind. Truly, the context of life is harder to consider than the singular events that lie between birth and death. However, the "between" is what matters most—the process of life that connects and blankets the events of our lives.

Generally speaking, the church has fallen victim to the same event-orientation—most significantly in regards to our salvation. Many consider and teach salvation as the initial event in the process—justification and reconciliation, redemption and rebirth. Salvation begins here, but there is so much more.

Most skip right to glorification—when we get to "go to heaven". That's a grand conclusion, but what about the parts "between" birth and death? Indeed, there is much process in the span of salvation, and there are a number of processes God employs to move us through the narrow gate and down the path that leads to eternal life (Matthew 7:13-14).

We have covered several of God's ways in previous chapters and will explore a few others here. But first, let's look at the evidence of salvation as a process.

> *For by grace you <u>have been saved</u> through faith, and that not of yourselves; it is the gift of God, not of works, lest anyone should boast (Ephesians 2:8-9).*

> *For the message of the cross is foolishness to those who are perishing, but to us who <u>are being saved</u> it is the power of God (1 Corinthians 1:18).*

> *For we are to God the fragrance of Christ among those who <u>are being saved</u> and among those who are perishing (2 Corinthians 2:15).*

> *Much more then, having now been justified by His blood, we shall be saved from wrath through Him. For if when we were enemies we were reconciled to God through the death of His Son, much more, having been reconciled, we <u>shall be saved</u> by His life (Romans 5:9-11).*

But he who endures to the end <u>shall be saved</u> (Matthew 24:13).

As followers of Jesus Christ, we "have been saved," we "are being saved," and we "shall be saved". The implications of this are profound. For example, how do you answer the question: "When were you saved?"

It makes you think, doesn't it? That's exactly what the Lord is after—followers who will consider the truth.

Many believe the initial event of their salvation will accomplish the fullness of the process. Consequently, enduring to the end does not fit their paradigm of "being saved". What if they unknowingly decide to avoid the enduring seasons? Will their houses withstand the storms and chaos?

Additionally, many in the church fail to consider, much less understand, that "we shall be saved by His life". An event will not save them, nor will a belief in that event. Our belief in Jesus' death and resurrection only begins the ongoing process of His life being manifested in us.

It seems to me this matter of salvation as a process should be discussed more often, and more broadly. The ramifications are significant. Eternal lives are hanging in the balance. Houses are at risk, and many are deceived.

The Process of Faith

The most fundamental way of God is the process of faith[3]. Indeed, God has embedded the process of faith into every

---

[3] The reader may recall a short reference to the process of faith in our exploration of reckoning on p. 48.

other process that involves humankind. It is perhaps God's greatest creation.

The process of faith is necessary for the whole and entirety of our Christian life. Having been saved through faith (Ephesians 2:8), we also discover we are to live by faith (Hebrews 10:38), to walk by faith (2 Corinthians 5:7), to fight the good fight of faith (1 Timothy 6:12), to take up the shield of faith (Ephesians 6:16), and to overcome the world by faith (1 John 5:4). Without faith it is impossible to please God (Hebrews 11:6). Whatever is not of faith is sin (Romans 14:23).

For the process of faith to be effectual, one must accept (with their mind) and believe (with their heart) that faith is a process. This will be difficult for many; for faith has become more of an event in the modern church; something akin to a decision, or choice (a mental exercise only).

While decision and choice are important parts of faith (faith is impossible without them), they are arguably the less important steps in the process. They seem more important to us because they are our biggest part.

For example, consider the "decision" people are encouraged to make for their salvation. Who allowed and orchestrated circumstances, and influenced the lives of people and principalities, to get the decision-maker to this point? Is it not the Holy Spirit Who convicts us of sin (John 16:8) and the Father Who draws a person to Christ (John 6:44)?

Furthermore, is that first and fateful decision the end of our salvation? Good heavens, let's hope not! Are we not being saved? Shall we not be saved? Indeed, faith is a journey, and not only for our ultimate salvation. God's purposes go far beyond the problem of our rebellion. We have been created as His workmanship, to walk in His good works (Ephesians 2:10).

God has provided (or will provide) faith for every commandment recorded in Scripture, and for those He speaks to us along the way (e.g., go to Africa, help that woman, stay away from that man). Every bit of faith begins with His word and ends with His good work—toward us, in us, and through us.

Think about that for a minute. Everything God and Jesus have commanded us to do, They do through the process of faith. This leaves us with one very basic and important question: how do we participate with them in that process? We participate in God's way for faith by following the three basic phases described in the Scriptures.

The Hearing of Faith:

> *And the disciples came and said to Him, "Why do You speak to them in parables?" He answered and said to them, "Because it has been given to you to know the mysteries of the kingdom of heaven, but to them it has not been given." (Matthew 13:10-11).*

The hearing of faith is the privilege of every disciple of Jesus Christ. Our King encourages us throughout the Gospels, "he who has ears to hear, let him hear!" and warns us through His messages to the seven churches of Revelation, "He who has an ear, let him hear what the Spirit says to the churches." Having ears to hear (and eyes to see) differentiates us from the world. Indeed, we should invest more time listening to the One who loves speaking with His children.

Obedience to the Faith:

> *Through Him we have received grace and apostleship for obedience to the faith among all nations for His name (Romans 1:5).*

Notice the preposition used here; it is more than a grammatical technicality that our obedience is "to the faith", and not "of the faith". Those who have been given the hearing of faith owe an obedient response **to** the faith that comes from God's word. Corporately, the carnal mind has done much to deceive and distract the people of God from our obedience to the faith. It is high time we gave more attention to this phase of the process.

The Work of Faith:

> *Therefore we also pray always for you that our God would count you worthy of this calling, and fulfill all the good pleasure of His goodness and the work of faith with power, that the name of our Lord Jesus Christ may be glorified in you, and you in Him, according to the grace of our God and the Lord Jesus Christ (2 Thessalonians 1:11-12).*

The work of faith is the good work of God which He created us to walk in. There is no need for controversy here. James speaks extensively about the relationship and purpose of work and faith. Jesus did the same; see the parable of the sheep and goats for one of many examples (Matthew 25:31-46). Here, Paul clarifies the work of faith is "with power". We could certainly use more of that kind of faith in these desperate days.

God's Way for Overcoming Lawlessness and Deception

*For the mystery of lawlessness is already at work...
(2 Thessalonians 2:7).*

Lawlessness has been around since Satan rebelled against God. It has plagued mankind since Adam and Eve succumbed to his deception and chose to follow his lead. The riots of 2020/2021 remind us that lawlessness is already at work.

For the children of God, the lawlessness we are experiencing can be a distraction, or it can become a warning of Satan's more insidious strategy and an encouragement to responsively step up our game. We would be wise to mount a proportional counter-offensive guided by the battle strategy revealed in this passage.

Sadly, most of us have become comfortable with some level of lawlessness in our lives. Who drives the speed limit anymore? For that matter, who loves their neighbor as themselves? Lawlessness is not a respecter of persons. Our comfort with it should cause great concern, perhaps even fear. Things could get worse.

Chapter Two of Paul's second letter to the Thessalonian church describes the tragic culmination of the legacy we have carried since mankind's rebellion in the Garden of Eden. It warns of a great apostasy, a falling away of people from the kingdom of God prior to Jesus' return and His gathering of the faithful to Himself.

Like me, you are probably wondering how a follower of Jesus Christ could ever leave Him. There are doctrines of man that argue against such a possibility. As you might imagine, such doctrines have become quite popular. Personally, I don't understand them; but exposing compromised doctrine is not our purpose here. Our purpose is to expose the enemy's tactics and encourage a sufficient response.

Lawlessness is simply a symptom of, and a cover for, the enemy's primary weapons. The rise of lawlessness is like smoke to a fire. Yes, the smoke can kill you, but the fire is the source. Put out the fire and the smoke will eventually abate.

> *The coming of the lawless one is according to the working of Satan, with all power, signs, and lying wonders, and with all unrighteous deception among those who perish because they did not receive the love of the truth, that they might be saved. And for this reason God will send them strong delusion, that they should believe the lie, that they all may be condemned who did not believe the truth but had pleasure in unrighteousness (2 Thessalonians 2:9-12).*

This passage explains and encourages God's way for protecting ourselves and those in our spheres of influence from Satan's power, signs, lying wonders, and unrighteous deception. Just to be clear, we are suggesting this response is as important today as it will be at the end of the Age. In fact, those who wait to the end will have little chance of mounting a defense.

Deception will overcome those who have not received a love of the truth, and this will happen WITH GOD'S HELP. Furthermore, that deception will prevent those poor individuals from being saved. There is no other way to interpret this passage. Let's begin by looking at "they did not receive the love of the truth" as the way to avoid deception.

First, the direct articles in this phrase are immensely important. There is a "the love" and a "the truth". There is not a variety of loves, nor a variety of truths that will protect us from deception. "The love" is *agapē*, the same love God has toward the world: sacrificial love. We are to love "the truth" sacrificially.

"The truth" (*alētheia*) is "what is true in any matter of consideration" (Outline of Biblical Usage, BlueLetterBible.org). As we understand, God defines what is true, and Jesus Christ embodies "the truth". Again, there are not a variety of truths, but many facets and expressions.

Lastly, to "receive" suggests something has been offered—a gift on the table. Do you find it difficult to motivate yourself to study your Bible? Do you ever wonder why others enjoy Christian podcasts, Sermonindex.com, and Precept studies? This sacrificial love for the truth cannot be created by man, nor imposed on another.

Those who love the truth have received the gift God offers to each one of us. Not just the truth, but love of it. Such love must be discovered and received, not manufactured. How could we refuse such an awesome gift? The love of the truth is a heart-tie with God.

The love of the truth is the first way of God for overcoming deception and lawlessness. The second and third are found in verse twelve: *"...that they all may be condemned who did not believe the truth but had pleasure in unrighteousness."*

Avoiding the destruction of our houses from deception and lawlessness requires more than receiving a love for the truth. Receiving must be followed by believing. Keep in mind that faith is also a gift of God (Ephesians 2:8). It comes by hearing, and hearing by the word of God (Romans 10:17). This begins a process—the process of faith—whereby we become obedient to the faith we have received, for the good work of faith God has created for us to walk in (Ephesians 2:10).

Lastly, strong houses must diligently resist the pleasures of unrighteousness. Unrighteous pleasure stands opposed to God's good pleasure and our belief in the truth. Unrighteousness and lawlessness go hand-in-hand. In the midst of lawlessness, we must remind ourselves and each other to overcome evil with good (Romans 12:21). Vengeance is unrighteous; forgiveness and blessing flow out from God's instruments of righteousness (v. 17-20).

In every battle and lawless uprising, we must resist the temptation to respond hastily to the external crisis and chaos of our day. Works without faith are not good works; they are sin (Romans 14:23). They will likely miss the mark. Feelings of urgency to respond must drive us to God—to receive (more) love of the truth, faith for the truth, and righteousness for a transformational response.

As disciple makers, we are challenged to be God's instruments of righteousness, offering the love of the truth. The urgency of the hour forces me to ask, "What does that look like for you in your spheres of influence? Is it anything different than the current interactions you have with those commissioned to your care? Have you received the love of the truth? How do you know?"

God's Way for Joyful, Spirit-filled Ministry

The process for finding joyful, Spirit-filled ministry, for both clergy and laypeople, is found in Psalm 37:4-6. We have explored this incredible passage, along with the process of transformation, beginning in Chapter Seven. I encourage it again here simply for the opportunity to testify of God's movement in the workplace to restore His church. God has positioned Christians in positions of authority to be strong houses, serving the Body of Christ as disciple-making transformation agents. *The Map Maker* (Streetman, 2015) explores the power of this process to produce joyful, Spirit-filled ministry where most people spend most of their working lives.

The ways of God are God's ways for the protection and maintenance of our spiritual houses. Choosing the ways of the world conforms us to systems and worldviews which are at enmity with God and threaten to reverse the restoration He has accomplished. To avoid this tragedy, we must become more disciplined in the ways of God. Indeed, practicing spiritual disciplines works hand-in-hand with God's ways, to secure and maintain our house.

Practicing Spiritual Disciplines

> *Therefore we must give the more earnest heed to the things we have heard, lest we drift away. For if the word spoken through angels proved steadfast, and every transgression and disobedience received a just reward, how shall we escape if we neglect so great a salvation (Hebrews 2:1-3)?*

Only a foolish man would expect his house to protect and maintain itself; discipline is required. Regrettably, the word discipline (and its application) has fallen out of favor in the modern church. We have lost appreciation for the spiritual disciplines God has provided for the protection and maintenance of our spiritual house.

Even the most fundamental disciplines are being neglected— disciplines that have been provided for our good. Seriously, where have the corporate prayer meetings and Bible studies gone? When was the last time someone encouraged you to practice solitude and silence, meditation, fasting, confession, or sacrifice? These were once considered fundamental exercises of our faith.

Several books which focus on the Christian disciplines have been included in the Recommended Reading list. I highly recommend each one. A short article on the disciplines God has provided for the process of faith can be found in the Appendix.

For our purposes, it is important we ensure our minds are rightly set in regards to the disciplines God has given us for our faith. We must therefore address a few potential deceptions.

First, the disciplines of God are not about merit. The disciplines are not "work" for our salvation or God's favor. Granted, practicing the disciplines will increase our faith, and thereby further our salvation, and we will experience more of God's favor through them. However—and this is BIG—they will be hay, wood, and stubble—totally ineffectual—if we are "working at it".

The disciplines have been given by God for the development of our relationship with Him—including the exercise of that relationship through us. The disciplines are God's ways for our participation with Him (Psalm 37:5). Our motivation in the disciplines must be to know God more and to be empowered with greater faith, the grace faith appropriates, and the effectual working of His grace in and through us.

Second, the disciplines are not about ability. Most of us will hear our carnal mind say, "I simply cannot do that", "I don't have time", or something similar. Like most deception, there is some truth in those statements; but, don't be put off. Here's what we should say back: "God has put His desire for this in my heart. He has the grace I need to do everything He desires. Let's see what He has to say about it." These words are alive and powerful truths (2 Corinthians 10:4; Hebrews 4:12-13).

Having put down our carnal mind, we can turn to God and work this out with Him. He will encourage, edify, and equip us for the desires He has put in our heart. He has promised to give it to us (Psalm 37:4).

Third, don't expect this to be easy. We must come back to God for encouragement, time and time again. That is His intention. He loves talking with His children. In the process, you will begin developing a key discipline—taking every thought captive to the obedience of Christ (2 Corinthians 10:5).

Along the way, the carnal mind will attempt to distract and deceive. It will even feign to help us through the process. Resist these temptations. It is better not to know what to do next—even to be in the worst kind of chaos—than to put our trust in something at enmity with God.

Fourth, there is no timetable for the mastery of the spiritual disciplines. Even the greatest mathematicians have to learn algebra and trigonometry before calculus. Similarly, there is an order to kingdom learning. It is perhaps unnecessary for some to study algebra or geometry for a full year. Others need more than one year of trigonometry.

The Holy Spirit will lead us to give the bulk of our time and energy to certain disciplines in particular seasons. For example, I have found great benefit for this season in setting my mind on things above instead of on social media. Additionally, there was a time when sports talk radio captivated my attention. I now cherish that time for prayer; and I have learned fasting as a discipline applies to more than food.

Finally, don't look for a program of disciplines. Resist them as the ways of man. Otherwise, we risk missing one of the greatest disciplines of all—walking in the Spirit (Galatians 5:16-26). Simply begin with the most important discipline of all: the quiet, listening, relational communication with God commonly known as prayer. Let Him lead you to the disciplines He has in mind for your good.

Neither Fearful nor Foolish

In times of uncertainty and chaos, it is important (and possible) for all Christians to avoid worldly fearfulness and carnal foolishness. This is particularly true of the Christians whom God has positioned with authority for leadership in the workplace. People in your spheres of influence will be looking to you for encouragement and example.

We pray people in your spheres of influence find many houses standing in the storm—as refuges of peace and sensibility. To that end, we humbly offer a few encouraging thoughts. These may not be new. Meditate on them nevertheless, recognizing they are also for the edification of those in your spheres of influence.

First, it will help you to know that chaos is normal for the Christian. Almost every book in the New Testament promises it. 2 Corinthians 3:18 is one of my favorite examples:

> *But we all, with unveiled face, beholding as in a mirror the glory of the Lord, are being transformed into the same image from glory to glory, just as by the Spirit of the Lord.*

It bears repeating, *metamorphoo* offers a perfect word picture for the process God employs to mature us as Christians. Anyone who has ever seen the inside of a cocoon knows what a mess it is for an ugly caterpillar to become a beautiful butterfly. This transformation is "by the Spirit of the Lord". In other words, the Holy Spirit is our transformer.

As leaders, we are blessed with the opportunity to be the vessel and instrument of God for the *metamorphoo* of those in our spheres of influence. Our only responsibility is to choose to participate in the work God is doing.

Second, it is particularly important in times of chaos to resist the temptation of turning to our carnal mind for advice. This is exactly what we have been taught for most of our lives. It is a lie and a deception. It is foolishness.

Every child of God has been blessed with access to heavenly wisdom.

> *But of Him you are in Christ Jesus, who became for us wisdom from God—and righteousness and sanctification and redemption—that, as it is written, "He who glories, let him glory in the Lord."* 1 Corinthians 1:30-31

> *For "who has known the mind of the Lord that he may instruct Him?" But we have the mind of Christ.* 1 Corinthians 2:16

Please, please, please, don't let your carnal mind convince you of anything else. We are being transformed by the renewing of our minds, by replacing our dependence on our carnal mind's reasoning with the wisdom of God in Christ Jesus. We have the mind of Christ! Now is a great time to start using it.

Third, where we start is critically and eternally important.

The fear of the LORD is the beginning of wisdom;
A good understanding have all those who do His
commandments.
His praise endures forever (Psalm 111:10).

Therefore, my beloved, as you have always obeyed, not as
in my presence only, but now much more in my absence,
work out your own salvation with fear and trembling; for
it is God who works in you both to will and to do for His
good pleasure (Philippians 2:13-14).

Therefore, since we are receiving a kingdom which cannot
be shaken, let us have grace, by which we may serve God
acceptably with reverence and godly fear. For our God is
a consuming fire (Hebrews 12:29-29).

There is a fear of God foundational to our awe and reverence of Him. That fear is the Greek *phobos*, which means "fear, dread, and terror"—a fear we must not ignore or avoid. The Spirit will help us find it. As Jesus sternly warned, we are to be fearful of God and not the world (Matthew 10:28). Indeed, the fear of the LORD protects us from foolishly fearing a world which has no power over us.

Yea, though I walk through the valley of the shadow of
death,
I will fear no evil;
For You are with me;
Your rod and Your staff, they comfort me (Psalm 23:4).

Lastly, during times like these, we are either grateful to know the voice of God or disappointed we have not given more attention to hearing from Him. In either case, now is a good time to spend more time with Him. In my humble opinion, our prayers must be more about hearing what God has to say about our storms and chaos than crying out for His help, even as we commit our houses to the refuge, encouragement, and ministry of others. He knows our needs before we ask. We need Him to reveal those needs to us.

God bless you with the godly fear that overcomes the world's fearfulness and your carnal mind's foolishness.

Conclusion

The practices and applications encouraged in this chapter are common and foundational to the normal Christian life. On the whole, had we been taught and encouraged to follow them from the onset of our walk with Christ, our houses would not have required restoration. In His grace and mercy, God has been persistent and longsuffering with His children.

The storms and chaos of this decade will prove the eternal value of God's faithfulness. Our reasonable response is surrender and sacrifice to His purposes (Romans 12:1): His reign, intimacy, and habitation with people in our spheres of influence. Indeed, God has strengthened our foundation and secured our structure for ministry to others. He would not have brought us this far had He not known the impact our ministry to others would have for His glory and kingdom. It is time to put out the welcome mat.

CHAPTER 11

Ministry to Others

By the time this book is published and read, the storms and chaos of the 2020s will be raging against our houses and those of people in our spheres of influence. Hopefully, God has graced you with enough time and courage for His inspection and restoration. If not, you should be looking around for the nearest strong house.

The inhabitants of that house will likely be expecting a knock at their door. If your house is standing, you should be expecting the same. In fact, you may have had a few pleas for help already. After all, this is one of God's primary purposes for the storms and chaos: to draw the Body of Christ together for His habitation.

You will recall from Chapter Three that restoring God's habitation is one of His eternal purposes. It is for this reason He never intends for us to do things in isolation. Standing strong in the storms will require community. This is another of God's ways that directly opposes the ways of man—particularly in our American society. In every worldly system (e.g., sports, business, government), the individual is recognized above the team. The man who is the captain of his own ship is praised and emulated. The "star" gets the big bucks.

This is not God's way! From the Old Testament, where God pleaded with His people not to desire a human king, to the

New Testament, where the Body of Christ becomes the Bride, the people of God are those who live in community, for the sake of building the fellowship of Christ. How are we to be made into the fellowship of the Father's habitation? Where do we start?

We start by searching it out: Beholding Christ as we seek the Holy Spirit's revelation and transformation (2 Corinthians 3:18). We will begin with Christ's prayer for our unity with one another.

> *I do not pray for these alone, but also for those who will believe in Me through their word; that they all may be one, as You, Father, are in Me, and I in You; that they also may be one in Us, that the world may believe that You sent Me. And the glory which You gave Me I have given them, that they may be one just as We are one: I in them, and You in Me; that they may be made perfect in one, and that the world may know that You have sent Me, and have loved them as You have loved Me (John 17:21-23).*

For over 2000 years, Christ has been praying from the desire of his heart for His Father to perfectly unite His disciples. He gave us the glory the Father gave Him for this very purpose!

Notice Christ asked His Father to make us one (not to help us do it). It is a work only the Father can accomplish. Our response must be agreement with Christ's prayer, and surrender to the Father's work. Those who resist will simply be left out.

Notice also our unity is God's way for successful evangelism. The spiritual connection between our unity and making disciples is a powerful one. The Father is answering His Son's prayer: His Bride will not be dismembered. Every purpose God has given us includes this underlying objective. Therefore, every purpose of God involves more than one person, and will by its nature draw more people to it.

The importance of our unity cannot be overstated: our salvation depends on it. This will come as a shock to some (and hopefully a sobering warning). Consider for a moment the following passages:

> For the wages of sin is death, but the gift of God is eternal life in Christ Jesus our Lord (Romans 6:23).

Eternal life is <u>in</u> Christ Jesus.

> For as we have many members in one body, but all the members do not have the same function, so we, being many, are one body in Christ, and individually members of one another (Romans 12:4-5).

We are one body—even members of one another—<u>in</u> Christ. The body of Christ and Christ are inseparable.

> I am the door. If anyone enters by Me, he will be saved, and will go in and out and find pasture (John 10:9).

Salvation comes through the door that is Christ. He is the only way <u>in</u>.

> Then one said to Him, "Lord, are there few who are saved?" And He said to them, "Strive to enter through the narrow gate, for many, I say to you, will seek to enter and will not be able (Luke 13:23-24).

Salvation comes to those who strive to enter <u>in</u>. Seeking to enter will not produce the desired result. In fact, desiring and hoping will end in frustration and disappointment. How many will be surprised when the books are opened (Revelation 20:12; Matthew 7:21-23)?

Now, let me ask you: Are you striving to enter into the community God has positioned around you? Do you know who they are? That community may be your family, your small group at church, your team at work, or your neighbors. It may be a combination, a blend of these, or some other form of community. God is very dynamic in this regard.

Striving to enter into your community is a strategic imperative for your (and their) entry into the kingdom of God. There simply is no entering without community. God has committed Himself to help you find and invest in your community, and a tool to help you discover your sphere of influence can be found in the Appendix.

The One Another Fellowship

So, now that we have the Holy Spirit's conviction and the Lord's perspective, let's move on to a deeper understanding of the fellowship He desires. We will do so by searching out the "one another" verses. As we review these, let the truth convict and encourage you in the potential of fellowship with "one another".

> *But if we walk in the light as He is in the light, we have fellowship with one another, and the blood of Jesus Christ His Son cleanses us from all sin (1 John 1:7).*

Fellowship with one another is evidence of our walk with Christ and prerequisite to His promise to cleanse us from all sin.

> *Salt is good, but if the salt loses its flavor, how will you season it? Have salt in yourselves, and have peace with one another (Mark 9:50).*

"Have peace with one another" is not an option; it is a command of our King. Note His use of the word "with". Our peace is found in intimate fellowship with one another, not in avoiding those we are uncomfortable to be around.

> *A new commandment I give to you, that you love one another; as I have loved you, that you also love one another (John 13:34).*

Another command: to love one another... as He loved us. Lest we forget, that love was sacrificial, even unto death on a cross.

> *So we, being many, are one body in Christ, and individually members of one another (Romans 12:5).*

Not only are we members of Christ's body, we are members of one another. How is that possible from a distance?

> *Be kindly affectionate to one another with brotherly love, in honor giving preference to one another (Romans 12:10).*

Giving preference means letting the other choose, not choosing for them. This type of love requires humility and trust in our heavenly Father.

Now may the God of patience and comfort grant you to be like-minded toward one another, according to Christ Jesus, that you may with one mind and one mouth glorify the God and Father of our Lord Jesus Christ (Romans 15:5-6).

One another fellowship empowers the renewal of our minds (i.e., transformation) through the communal submission to the mind of Christ. We become unified in thought and worship.

Now therefore, it is already an utter failure for you that you go to law against one another. Why do you not rather accept wrong? Why do you not rather let yourselves be cheated (1 Corinthians 6:7)?

Our ill-treatment of one another in the public square brings shame to Jesus Christ and the rest of His Body. Our acceptance of being wronged protects Him and His Body.

For you, brethren, have been called to liberty; only do not use liberty as an opportunity for the flesh, but through love serve one another (Galatians 5:13).

One of the saddest things to see are church fellowships in close geographic proximity living apart from one another. Rather than serve each other, they glory in themselves. We are called to a much higher witness of God's love for one another.

I, therefore, the prisoner of the Lord, beseech you to walk worthy of the calling with which you were called, with all lowliness and gentleness, with longsuffering, bearing with one another in love, endeavoring to keep the unity of the Spirit in the bond of peace (Ephesians 4:1-3).

Our worth as followers of Jesus Christ is measured by our bearing with one another in love and unity.

> *And let us consider one another in order to stir up love and good works, not forsaking the assembling of ourselves together, as is the manner of some, but exhorting one another, and so much the more as you see the Day approaching (Hebrews 10:24-25).*

The issue is not how we assemble—from small groups to large denominations—but the heart we have for each other as we assemble. Is our desire for ourselves and our group, or for something greater? To fight the temptations of sectarianism, we must be intentional about our assembling together in love for the whole Body of Christ.

> *Finally, all of you be of one mind, having compassion for one another; love as brothers, be tenderhearted, be courteous; not returning evil for evil or reviling for reviling, but on the contrary blessing, knowing that you were called to this, that you may inherit a blessing (1 Peter 3:8-9).*

Our love for one another is no less than our calling and the source of our inheritance in Christ. This alone should be enough motivation to allow God to make us into the one another fellowship He desires.

Sacrifice in Chaos—A Christian Distinctive

When inLight Consulting was coming into focus, several well-meaning workplace ministers counseled me to lead with something other than surrender, sacrifice, and submission. Had I been more than God's instrument, the ministry of inLight Consulting might have followed their advice. But God would not have it. He insisted on the truth: Christian leadership requires counter-cultural sacrifice. At no other time is this more evident than in the midst of storms and chaos.

To their credit, the workplace ministers I surveyed were right in a way. The call to sacrifice has been a particularly difficult message for workplace leaders to hear.

Perhaps a bit of context would be helpful. inLight was formed to help Christian leaders find joyful, Spirit-filled ministry in the workplace, by becoming disciple-making transformation agents. Joyful, Spirit-filled ministry begins with surrender to the desires God has deposited into our hearts. It ends with the good work He created for us to supernaturally walk in, as we submit to the Holy Spirit.[4]

The preparatory journey from desire to good work requires sacrifice and includes chaos; the two go hand in hand (remember *metamorphoo*). God sent His Son to lead us through the process.

> *Then Jesus said to them, "Follow Me, and I will make you become fishers of men." They immediately left their nets and followed Him (Mark 1:17-18).*

The first of many requirements for becoming a disciple of Jesus Christ is to follow Him. Only in the following can we be made. We know from Philippians 2:5-8 that Jesus' time here on Earth began, ended, and was filled with sacrifice. This is the path He has called us to follow—a path of storms and chaos.

---

[4] The key Biblical references include Psalm 37:4-6; 2 Corinthians 3:18; Romans 12:2; Ephesians 2:10; and Matthew 5:16. Reckoning the truth of these is a highly profitable exercise.

These things I have spoken to you, that in Me you may have peace. In the world you will have tribulation; but be of good cheer, I have overcome the world (John 16:33).

So Jesus said to them again, "Peace to you! As the Father has sent Me, I also send you." (John 20:21).

There are two encouragements to draw from these verses—both relating to opportunity. First, there is the opportunity of need. The chaos that has found its way into our lives has created, and will continue to create, opportunities for us to exercise the sacrificial love of God. There is no love of God that is not sacrificial. The cost of opportunity is not a burdensome investment we must make, but the loss of missed opportunity to sacrificially love one another. This is counter to worldly thinking and is therefore a Christian distinctive.

Secondly, there is the opportunity for preparation. There is simply no way around it: transformation requires sacrifice. The path that leads to eternal life is difficult (Matthew 7:14). We must strive to enter in (Luke 13:24). Only those who will lose their life for Jesus' sake will find it (Matthew 16:25). God uses storms and chaos to identify and shake free those things which do not belong (e.g., greed, fear, pride); and to increase those things which make us more glorified instruments of His grace (e.g., faith, peace, humility).

The world cannot understand this work of God in our pursuit of self-sacrifice; it is counter to their culture (and therefore, a Christian distinctive). However, those who have been given eyes to see will be drawn to the refuge and encouragement of your house. Please, please, please, do not miss this providential opportunity to develop and express the counter-cultural, Christianly distinctive sacrifice in the storms and chaos of this decade. You were created for it!

Strong Houses are Recognized by Their Doing

After putting three screws in my hip, the doctor told me how to take care of it. He said if I did the necessary work, I would get 95-98% of my functionality and strength back. For nine long weeks I had to use a walker to avoid putting weight on that leg. Using that walker was painful, aggravating, and inhibiting.

Six weeks after my surgery, the doctor told me to start seeing a physical therapist. Three weeks later, the physical therapist told me to start using crutches and bearing weight on the injured leg; beginning with 50 percent, and increasing gradually over the next six weeks. He also told me about the stretches and exercises I could do at home to strengthen my hip and the atrophied supporting muscles. Eventually, he told me to put the crutches down and walk normally.

Now, what do you think would have happened if I had been a hearer of what the doctor and physical therapist said, but not a doer? According to the doctor, it would have been absolutely disastrous. If I had, in my aggravation, tried to walk too soon, I would have broken the hip again—resulting in another surgery to replace it entirely. If I had not later started walking, stretching and exercising, my muscles would have atrophied further and I would have gotten necrosis of the bone.

Fortunately, I am—like most of you—a good hearer and doer when it comes to my health. The result: I am riding my bike as long and far as I was before the accident. By doing what I heard, I have made it back to at least 90 percent of my functionality and strength in less than six months. I am confident I will get my health back to the doctor's optimistic number.

My doctor and physical therapist assumed I would be a wise doer of what each one had to say. Jesus had something similar to say about being a doer:

> *Therefore whoever hears these sayings of Mine, and does them, I will liken him to a wise man who built his house on the rock: and the rain descended, the floods came, and the winds blew and beat on that house; and it did not fall, for it was founded on the rock (Matthew 7:24-25).*

What would it mean for your house to stand in the storm? What would it mean for your family, fellowship, and community? It will mean far more than being able to ride a bicycle again. Far more!

Why do we take the directions of our doctors and physical therapists more seriously than the commands of our King? Are the consequences any less disastrous? Consider what James has to say:

> *But be doers of the word, and not hearers only, deceiving yourselves. For if anyone is a hearer of the word and not a doer, he is like a man observing his natural face in a mirror; for he observes himself, goes away, and immediately forgets what kind of man he was. But he who looks into the perfect law of liberty and continues in it, and is not a forgetful hearer but a doer of the work, this one will be blessed in what he does (James 1:22-25).*

Self-deception, forgetfulness regarding the kind of people we are (i.e., the people of God), and the loss of blessing in our work are the consequences of being only hearers. James goes on to say even faith must be worked out in ministry to others to avoid becoming dead (James 2:14-17). The Holy Spirit once shared with me, as I was cycling past some particularly pungent roadkill, "That is what dead faith smells like in God's nostrils."

Our spiritual health is more important than the health of our bodies (1 Timothy 4:8). The words of our King are far more important than that of our doctors. We are being deceived to think otherwise. The consequences of our failure to be doers are enormous and tragic. Indeed, failing to do the will of God threatens our eternal security.

> *Not everyone who says to Me, "Lord, Lord," shall enter the kingdom of heaven, but he who does the will of My Father in heaven. Many will say to Me in that day, "Lord, Lord, have we not prophesied in Your name, cast out demons in Your name, and done many wonders in Your name?" And then I will declare to them, "I never knew you; depart from Me, you who practice lawlessness!" (Matthew 7:21-23).*

This may be the hardest saying to hear in the entire Sermon on the Mount. Many have gone to great lengths to explain away its meaning. Why? Because it reveals a facet of God's character that many would prefer not to consider: His severity. We do so at our own peril.

> *Therefore consider the goodness and severity of God: on those who fell, severity; but toward you, goodness, if you continue in His goodness. Otherwise you also will be cut off (Romans 11:22).*

Our God is a just God (Psalm 7:11). This is one of the things we like about God—when He is just on our behalf, or just against the wicked. What we don't like to consider—nor communicate—is the just rebuke, chastening and scourging of our loving Father and Savior (Hebrews 12:5-11; Revelations

3:19). Considering such things makes us uncomfortable and concerned about our relationship with God. It may even cause us to work out our salvation with fear and trembling (Philippians 2:12). Imagine that!

When Jesus says something in a straightforward way—as in this passage—we should take Him at His word. Think about it. He did not come to trick us with the truth. Why would He say something about a topic as important as entering the kingdom, in a way that might mislead His followers? It just doesn't make sense.

So, just how do we do the will of our Father in heaven? The answer is simple: We surrender to His will.

> *If anyone wills to do His will, he shall know concerning the doctrine, whether it is from God or whether I speak on My own authority (John 7:17).*

This is, of course, easier said than done. It includes, but is more than, putting aside our personal desires. It is embracing His will for every moment of our lives—even when we don't know what His will is going to be. The only way for us to know we are doing the will of God (and shall enter the kingdom of heaven) is to trust Him completely.

This is important: That means refusing to trust in anyone else. ANYONE ELSE! Please, please, please, don't dismiss this. It is a severe truth; and it is something worth fighting for.

In closing, be encouraged in the knowledge that God has put the desire to do His will in our hearts. He has promised to give us that desire (Psalm 37:4), when we surrender to the work He is doing in us—to will and to do for His good pleasure (Philippians 2:13). His good pleasure is to give us His kingdom (Luke 12:32).

God bless you with the grace to surrender.

Strong Houses and Their Wealth

Strong houses are blessed by God to become His instruments of refuge, understanding, and encouragement. The privilege and responsibility will inevitably challenge our sense of security, threaten our treasure, and test our allegiance to God and our love for others. Whether we have much or little, the opportunity to sacrificially share our wealth will come.

For some of us, this will be the most trying and uncomfortable test. The best thing we can do ahead of any test is prepare our hearts and minds, being careful to appreciate our enemies' capabilities for deception and distraction. While every opportunity will require a prayerful hearing from God, we will benefit greatly from a preemptive examination of our heart and a renewing of our mind in the truth.

To begin, let me establish a baseline for the meaning of "wealth". Here are some statistics I have discovered over the years:

- According to the Federal Reserve's Survey of Consumer Finances (Bricker et al., 2017), the median net worth of all U.S. families is $97,300. Plugging this number into the Global Rich List calculator (n.d.), we discover the average American family has more wealth than almost 92% of everyone else in the world. In other words, more than half of all Americans are ten-percenters.
- A U.S. worker making the federally mandated minimum wage ($7.25/hour) earns more salary than

92.2% of workers in the rest of the world (Global Rich List calculator, n.d.).

The statistics do not lie: the vast majority of Americans are "wealthy" when compared to the rest of the world—including most of our Christian brethren. These stats don't tell the whole story, but they do help us appreciate what God has entrusted to those of us who live in the United States of America.

Now, allow me to trouble you with two passages of Scripture. The first has haunted me for years now:

> *By this we know love, because He laid down His life for us. And we also ought to lay down our lives for the brethren. But whoever has this world's goods, and sees his brother in need, and shuts up his heart from him, how does the love of God abide in him? My little children, let us not love in word or in tongue, but in deed and in truth. And by this we know that we are of the truth, and shall assure our hearts before Him (1 John 3:16-19).*

I suspect the Holy Spirit, writing through John, does not intend for our understanding of "brother" to be limited by borders. How many of us desire to know the needs of our brothers and sisters around the world, much less open our hearts to them? Have we considered the jeopardy we have introduced into our walk with Christ?

The second passage we must consider is the Parable of the Talents (Matthew 25:14-30). Please read it in light of Jesus' warning against the deceitfulness and danger of riches.

> *Now he who received seed among the thorns is he who hears the word, and the cares of this world and **the***

189

deceitfulness of riches choke the word, and he becomes unfruitful (Matthew 13:22).

*Then Jesus said to His disciples, "Assuredly, I say to you that **it is hard for a rich man to enter the kingdom of heaven**. And again I say to you, it is easier for a camel to go through the eye of a needle than for a rich man to enter the kingdom of God." (Matthew 19:23-24).*

My conviction is this: wealth that is not completely submitted to the reign of God is a curse to humankind. Our salvation hangs in the balance over the heart and mind we have toward our wealth.

Furthermore, "talents" certainly include whatever wealth God has entrusted to us. The return He expects from that investment must be something of value to Him and His kingdom—not our comfort and security until He calls us home.

Just to be clear, we are not suggesting to "forsake all that he has" (Luke 14:33) means to give everything away and live in a state of poverty. God entrusts us to be good stewards of something; and He uses our stewardship to mature us in Christ and community. The well-being of my wife and children—even after my death—is part of that responsibility.

Furthermore, there is Romans 14:23 (*"whatever is not from faith is sin"*); and Jesus' sobering warning in Matthew 7:21.

Not everyone who says to Me, "Lord, Lord," shall enter the kingdom of heaven, but he who does the will of My Father in heaven.

Obviously, whatever we do with the wealth entrusted to us, it must be done in the Father's will, and it must be done in faith. Consequently, we must be able to hear His voice and His word for faith to invest wisely in His kingdom. He promises we will know the truth if we are submitted to His will (John 7:17). For this reason, we are encouraged to ask the hard questions now.

> *Therefore, my beloved, as you have always obeyed, not as in my presence only, but now much more in my absence, work out your own salvation with fear and trembling; for it is God who works in you both to will and to do for His good pleasure (Philippians 2:12-13).*

In the spirit of Philippians 2:12-13, answer the following questions for yourself. Use them as conversation starters with God. Allow Him to challenge you and soften your heart for our brethren around the world. Allow the truth to set you free from conformity with the world and to transform you by the renewing of your mind (Romans 12:2).

1. Why has the Lord given us such wealth when so many of our brethren are living in poverty?
2. Why would God give it to us and not to them? What have we done that we should live so far above another child of God?
3. Has He not given it to us to invest in the things important to Him?
4. Are we burying our talents?
5. Has God given us this wealth to prove where our true devotions lie? How far are we from believing the prosperity gospel?
6. Can we enter in through the narrow gate with so much coinage in our pockets?
7. What do we believe about this?

If the chaos we are experiencing continues much further, many in the American church will soon lose much of the wealth entrusted to them. When the housing bubble burst in 2008, that was roughly 30 percent of all the savings of every Christian in America. All of it LOST! I wonder how much of that was intended for eternal investment, never to be lost, returning a profit for eternity.

Thank you for your attention to this issue. I believe it has been God's mercy to hold it to the last section of this last chapter. I pray you can hear my heart in it. Better yet, I hope and pray you will hear the heart of our Father.

Conclusion

Sacrificial ministry to one another sets the followers of Jesus Christ apart from the rest of the world. Regrettably, our failure in this area has produced a forgetfulness of who we are, both individually and corporately. There is no better time than in storms and chaos for the church of Jesus Christ to remember who we were created to be. As vessels, instruments, and weapons of God, we have much to offer. Strong houses are recognized by their love for the brethren. Communities of strong houses are like cities set on a hill—a light to the world. The world will know us by our sacrificial love for one another, and they will be drawn to the refuge, encouragement, and salvation of our King.

Epilogue—Focus, Perspective, and a Prayer

Maintaining Our Focus

As the storm clouds gather and your urgency for preparation ramps up, you may discover you are having a harder time maintaining focus on the spiritual side of your preparation. While it is important to be physically prepared (as much as the Lord and His wisdom have directed you), we must not allow those concerns to supersede the spiritual preparation required for the days ahead. This is critical for you, for those in your spheres of influence, and (most importantly) for the kingdom of God.

We must keep, at the forefront, God's desires to make us His instruments of refuge, truth, and encouragement to those He has gathered around us. The coming decade will provide an incredible opportunity for ministry to the lost and wandering children of God. I hope and pray the following reminders will encourage, edify, and equip you in your spiritual preparation.

Let me share two additional thoughts before you consider this list. First, there is nothing here we should not be doing anyway. Second, God knows you cannot do all this at once. He will direct you, by His Spirit, to the one(s) that will be most profitable to His kingdom.

- **Do "these sayings of Mine"** – The most obvious thing we can do to prepare for any storm is to follow Jesus' instruction for building a strong house (Matthew 7:24-27). How can we do what we do not know? Begin by prayerfully reading the Sermon on the Mount, in Matthew 5-7 and Luke 6 (a read through takes less than twenty minutes). Trust that the Sermon does not contain a set of Christian requirements, but instead describes the person into whom the Godhead desires to transform you (read that again).

- **Find the center of God's will for this season** – God is always orchestrating for His purposes: to restore His reign over, intimacy with, and habitation in His people. The desires for these things are also in your heart. Find them and surrender to them.

- **Believe and reckon Ephesians 6:10** – *Be strong in the Lord, and in the power of His might.* Grace has been given for our obedience to this command. Our strength comes from an abiding relationship with Him. How do we abide? The answer can be found in John 15 (the whole chapter). Furthermore, the "power of His might" is the authority Jesus Christ has been given to reign over all things. Coming under that authority gives us strength for the storm.

- **Check your armor** – Continuing in Ephesians 6, we recognize our armor is for "the evil day" (v. 13). We also recognize each piece of armor is a description of what Jesus Christ is to His followers. He is our salvation, peace, faith, etc. Make a prayerful assessment of your armor. Put on Christ!

- **Begin practicing Philippians 4:4-7** – These verses are God's prescription for peace. Practicing the process now will renew your mind to go there when the chaos of the storm begins. Ask God to reveal your fears and anxieties about the future. Now is the time to deal with them. What Satan intends for evil, God will turn to good. God will set you free from the fears of this life, to walk in His victories.

- **Let the possibilities excite you** – The days ahead will provide many opportunities for the followers of Jesus Christ to be all we have desired to be: to love the LORD with our all and our neighbors as ourselves; to give what we have of the world's goods to those who are in need; to lay down our lives for the brethren; to please our Master by investing our talents wisely; etc.
- **Diligently strive to enter the kingdom** – Read 2 Peter 1:5-11 and Luke 13:23-27. No one can be diligent and strive for you; and you cannot do either of these things for anyone else. We must turn our hearts to the One who can; and we must encourage one another.

Let me remind you: You are the leaders God has chosen for this season. By His grace and wisdom, you will be His mighty men, women and children in the coming storms. He will use you to protect and train others. I am truly blessed to be in this great adventure with you.

Maintaining Our Perspective

One does not need prophetic gifts to recognize the chaos and storms of 2020 will continue for the foreseeable future. The 2020s will likely be the most chaotic time most of us (at least in America) will experience in our lifetime. Translating this into "kingdom-speak": this decade will be the most opportunistic and pivotal time the God-assigned ambassadors to the United States of America have seen in almost 100 years.

There is no better time to be a disciple maker than in the midst of chaos and storms. If our houses remain standing, many who have lost theirs will be coming to us for refuge, encouragement, and understanding. With this great opportunity in mind, I offer you three considerations:

Perspective: We are seated with Christ in heavenly places, with access to Heaven's perspective (Ephesians 2:6). Though we may be physically buffeted, in the spirit realm we look down on the storm and chaos with confidence in God's purpose, and the peace it provides.

Furthermore, strong houses are built from an eternal perspective; they are built to last. The trials and tribulations of this season will pass. We must keep our eyes on the prize and faithfully run the race set before us.

Position: God providentially positions us geographically, relationally, and with particular responsibilities. Consideration for the impact zone of these dimensions is critical. Our influence will be greatest (for God's glory) with people in our closest spheres.

We must avoid and reject the temptation to give unbalanced attention to people and situations on our periphery (e.g., political wrangling in Washington, D.C., and riots on the other side of the country).

Privilege: We are ambassadors of a kingdom far greater than the United States of America (2 Corinthians 5:20). This will be controversial, but it seems to me we must choose between remaining a citizen of America or becoming God's ambassador to it. God does not entertain split allegiances.

Furthermore, God has made us vessels, instruments, and weapons of righteousness (Romans 6:13; 2 Timothy 2:21). We are stewards of the mysteries of God, required to be found faithful (1 Corinthians 4:1-2). These are privileges, not burdens. They represent opportunities to experience the glory of God in the good work He has created for us to walk in (Ephesians 2:10; Matthew 5:16).

Developing and maintaining the proper perspective of our position and privilege as Kingdom citizens and ambassadors in this world will sustain and empower us through the chaos and storms of the 2020s. God will use us to encourage, edify, and equip others for the same.

A Prayer for Your Encouragement and Power

In closing, let me pray for you…

> … *that the God of our Lord Jesus Christ, the Father of glory, may give to you the spirit of wisdom and revelation in the knowledge of Him, the eyes of your understanding being enlightened; that you may know what is the hope of His calling, what are the riches of the glory of His inheritance in the saints, and what is the exceeding greatness of His power toward us who believe, according to the working of His mighty power which He worked in Christ when He raised Him from the dead and seated Him at His right hand in the heavenly places. (Ephesians 1:17-20).*

There is a power that has exceeding greatness towards those who believe; the power of God toward the church. This is the same power that raised Christ from the dead and seated Him at the Father's right hand. It is the same power that works in us to will and to do for His good pleasure (Philippians 2:13); and the same that is able to do exceedingly, abundantly above all we can ask or think (Ephesians 3:20).

The power God has toward the church is the power that will prepare you for the storm and empower you to help others prepare!

Jesus exercised this power and commissioned His followers to do the same (John 14:12; 20:21). As we submit to His power, the Holy Spirit transforms us into instruments and weapons of righteousness; for the transformation of those in our spheres of influence. In so doing, the glory of God is manifested.

Do not be deceived. His power is not given out like rechargeable batteries, requiring us to go back and get recharged. It is not something we own, to carry around in our independent selves. The power of God is in the life of Jesus; indwelling us for the glory of our Father in heaven (Matthew 5:16).

Be strong in the Lord, and in the power of His might; for our God is exceedingly greater than we can imagine!

Humbly yours and forever His,

Appendix

The Sayings of Jesus

The Beatitudes (Matthew 5:1-12)

From poor in spirit to rejoicing when persecuted, the Beatitudes invite the followers of Jesus Christ to live as no mortal can. And yet, they describe the normal Christian life—the life God will make in us, if we will surrender, sacrifice, and submit ourselves to His working.

Salt and Light (Matthew 5:13-16)

In this saying, Jesus moves from describing the character of a kingdom citizen—states of being that are only possible through His life—to the way a citizen of the kingdom lives out the normal Christian life. It turns out "let" is a powerful word in the kingdom of God.

Jesus Fulfills the Law (Matthew 5:17-20)

In this short declaration, Jesus establishes the foundation on which the remaining sermon will stand. Battle lines had been drawn. The old guard had been put on notice: the kingdom and its King were in their midst, and religious oppression was not His way. Indeed, He had come to set the captives free (Luke 4:18-19).

Guard Your Tongue (Matthew 5:21-22)

One of the more subtle and pervasive worldly deceptions can be found in the way Christians use their tongues. What we hear in the world tends to find its way into our vocabulary. In between the hearing and the saying, our minds are at risk of being conformed to the world.

Be Reconciled (Matthew 5:23-26)

This saying is about as straight forward as they come: if anyone, brother or adversary, has something against you, do all in your power to be reconciled with them. In the kingdom, alienation invalidates our offering to God (see Romans 12:2). In the world, it simply does not end well for us; nor for those who depend on us. We must trust God to protect us as we pursue reconciliation in the way Jesus has instructed.

Guard Your Heart (Matthew 5:27-28)

The house who stands in the storm will be the house of the man or woman who guards their heart from the lusts of their eyes. This is an incredibly important issue for the church in America; particularly when you consider the houses who are being built around our pastors and our fellowships.

Be Serious about Sin (Matthew 5:29-30)

Sin in the individual is sin in the camp. Both are serious matters for a church fellowship—particularly in this season of approaching storms. The church fellowships who fail to administer discipline are weakening their house; making it susceptible to a great fall.

Fear the Consequences of Divorce (Matthew 5:31-32)

The extent we, the children of God, have adopted the world's way for the marriage covenant is tragic. Perhaps one must accept there are no exceptional circumstances. However, how grieved God must be over the compromise that has entered the church. At the risk of sounding harsh, most divorce in the church happens because the children of God do not seriously consider this passage before and during their marriage.

Do Not Swear at All (Matthew 5:33-37)

Could anything be more clear? Whatever is more than our "yes" and "no" is from the evil one. Why then do so many followers of Jesus Christ submit to the courts of this nation, put one hand on a Bible, raise the other, and swear to tell the whole truth and nothing but the truth? Is this not taking an oath? Does it make it okay—or does it make it worse—that a Bible is used in this process?

Overcome Evil with Good (Matthew 5:38-41)

Citizens of the kingdom of God give up their personal rights. Jesus is encouraging us to shift our perspective back to that of the bondservant and child; to give up our rights and trust God in the face of evil; so that He can use us as instruments of His love, goodness, and glory.

Give and Lend (Trust and Obey) (Matthew 5:42)

This verse is pivotal in our discussion and obedience to "these sayings of mine" in the Sermon on the Mount and beyond. We are tempted to move on to "easier" sayings. But if we start now, I guarantee most of the rest will go in the same direction; and habits are hard to break. Perhaps now is the time to face our fears and deal with the reality of our commitment to faith and obedience.

Love, Bless, Do Good, and Pray for Your Enemies (Matthew 5:43-45)

In this case, Jesus is addressing a humanly devised extension of the Law which was not intended by God. While they were told to love their neighbor (Leviticus 19:18), God never commanded His people to conversely hate their enemies. It must have been quite a challenge to the people of Jesus' day to learn the desire of God's heart for His children is love, blessing, goodness, and prayer for their enemies.

Be Extraordinary; Be Perfect (Matthew 5:46-48)

As you can see, Jesus expects we shall be perfect, just as our Father in heaven is perfect. Whether you believe this is a possibility for this life, or reserved for the next, it is the destination Jesus has in mind; and destinations require journeys. Connecting this to our treatment of others in this life makes it clear we are in the process of being perfected.

Resist the Enemy's Temptations (Matthew 6:1-4)

Our flesh is fed by the praise of others (two forces working together). Our unrenewed mind reasons, "Why shouldn't our charitable deeds be noticed? They are good examples for others." The obvious answer is "because Jesus said so", and that is enough; but it is not all we have been given to understand. In the kingdom of God, there is enmity between God and the world. He will not mix His reward with the rewards of the world.

Do Things God's Way (Matthew 6:5-6)

In this passage, Jesus Christ has given precise step-by-step instructions for the way we are to pray. The simple fact He has prescribed a process for our prayer life is significant. This leads us to the underlying "to do" of this passage: Do things God's way.

Learn to Pray (Matthew 6:5-13)

The disciple was asking for more than instruction in prayer. He recognized Jesus' way of prayer is so far removed from their own that what they had been calling prayer might as well have been called "apple". Jesus' way of prayer was about life and relationship. It availed much.

Forgive Their Trespasses (Matthew 6:14-15)

This may be the most direct, easily understood and often taught saying of Jesus. So, why is the church so divided over the trespasses of others? It is tragically ironic such a saying—and the consequences of not doing it—has had so little response in the church. Perhaps the easy once-saved-always-saved gospel has turned this saying of Jesus into an option.

Fast to Please God (Matthew 6:16-18)

It is interesting, revelatory, and convicting that Jesus speaks of fasting in the same way He spoke of doing good and praying. In doing so, He is making it clear for us that fasting is to be a very important part of the normal Christian life.

Lay Up Treasures in Heaven (Matthew 6:19-21)

Some sayings are difficult to do, simply because we have a hard time hearing them. This saying is particularly hard to hear for those in the church who are tempted—and even presently deceived—by the American Dream.

Get Focused; Stay Focused (Matthew 6:22-24)

Jesus is after more than checklist obedience. He came to save that which was lost, to build His church, and to commission disciples. He intends to lead us, make us, and use us to make others. Such a life requires more than passive or casual compliance. Disciples are disciplined, focused on the mission, and focused on one Master.

Do Not Worry about Your Life (Matthew 6:25-34)

The word "therefore" is placed strategically throughout the Bible. Because we cannot serve two masters—particularly God and treasures—we must stop worrying about our life. Once again, we have a saying of Jesus we are to do by not doing. Once again, we are faced with a seemingly impossible task.

Judge Not (Matthew 7:1-2)

This passage has been a challenge to many in the church. Many have harmed themselves (and the church) by misinterpreting this to mean we are prohibited from identifying the sin in our brother and helping him to remove it.

Get the Plank Out (Matthew 7:3-5)

In this saying of Jesus, we learn the process for helping our brothers and sisters find the grace to live a life without sin, for his benefit and that of the church. That process begins with each one of us dealing with our own sin.

Be Discerning AND Selective in Sharing the Truth (Matthew 7:6)

Jesus anticipated His followers would be tempted to offer holy and precious things to the wrong people. To avoid the resulting calamity, we must develop a more intimate relationship with God and with those who come into our spheres of influence.

Ask, Seek, and Knock (Matthew 7:7-8)

We know Jesus is not a liar. There must be something more; something Jesus is assuming we understand in this saying. Hopefully, understanding will help us be better doers; and help us appropriate His promises of getting, finding, and entering.

Trust God for More (Matthew 7:9-11)

Jesus realized His sayings would be a challenge to His followers—even to those with the strongest faith. He knew it would be hard for us to see beyond this world and this life; that our paradigms are insidiously constrained by our current realities.

Take the Initiative for Good (Matthew 7:12)

Here we have what many call "The Golden Rule". Well, not exactly. In fact, it is very different from, "Do unto others as you would have them do unto you." That version suggests our motivation to treat others well is our own well-being. That is not what Jesus is trying to say.

Enter by the Narrow Gate (Matthew 7:13-14)

There was a time when this saying of Jesus was well known to all Christians; now, perhaps not. Even those of us who have heard it many times have failed to grasp—or have lost—the gravity of its meaning. Entering the kingdom of God is not as easy as we would like to think; nor communicate.

Beware the False Prophets (Matthew 7:15-16)

It is helpful for our understanding to recognize and consider the Sermon on the Mount as more than a collection of sayings. The order is important. Jesus warned of false prophets immediately following His saying about the narrow gate and difficult way. He did so to help us understand what would be false about them.

Bear Good Fruit (Matthew 7:17-20)

Bearing good fruit is a test for every tree, not just prophets and teachers. In fact, our faithfulness as disciples of Jesus Christ is evidenced by our bearing much fruit (John 15:8). To do otherwise results in our being cut down (or cut off) and thrown into the fire.

Do the Will of My Father in Heaven (Matthew 7:21-23)

This may be the hardest saying to hear in the entire Sermon on the Mount. Many have gone to great lengths to explain away its meaning. Why? Because it reveals a facet of God's character many would prefer not to consider: His severity. We do so at our own peril.

Do Them (Matthew 7:24-27)

As we come to the end of Matthew's account of the Sermon on the Mount, we find ourselves faced with a few challenging questions: If you don't know the sayings of Jesus, how can you hear them? If you cannot hear them, how can you do them? If you do not do them, what will be the state of your house?

The Sermon on the Mount in Luke's Gospel

Luke's shorter presentation of the Sermon on the Mount enriches Matthew's account by adding a down-to-earth harmony for the similar sayings. He also shares several new sayings, including the sobering "woes" of Luke 6:24-26.

House Fire Chaos and Blessing

We must through many tribulations enter the kingdom of God (Acts 14:22).

This is a story about a family who was burned out of their house, and the journey God orchestrated to bless them in their tribulation. It is a story about a tragedy that was turned to adventure—through the supernatural grace of God. More than anything, it is a story of God's unfailing and extravagant love!

There are many types and degrees of tribulation. A house fire is a dramatic event that draws a lot of attention. However, we want to recognize it does not compare to losing a spouse or child, getting cancer, losing your business, or many other difficult situations that befall the human race.

The "level" of our tribulation was established by God to manifest His glory and transform us more into the image of Christ. Others are honored and trusted with greater, and lesser, tribulation. Our hearts go out to those whose trials go on for years—even lifetimes. It is our prayer that these, and others, will be encouraged by our testimony of the Father's faithfulness and His extravagant love.

While this story is not intended to be a spiritual lesson, we pray others will learn from our experience. We know the wisdom and revelation we were given in the journey is to be applied elsewhere; and not just for ourselves. In fact, God has given us a message for the church. We have titled it "Chaos Navigation", and offer it to anyone who is interested. For ourselves, we are still applying the lessons learned—being taught through its application in some new experiences.

As a last word of preface, let it be known Beth, Sarah, Matthew, and I have not "deserved" or "earned" anything we had before the fire, anything we now have, or anything we've been given during this journey. Even the "right" decisions we made are a result of the Lord's grace in teaching us how to hear His voice, trust Him, and obey His instruction.

Tragedy and the Supernatural

On April 18, 2009, Beth and I were returning from dinner when we received a phone call from our son, Matthew. At first, we couldn't understand him. Thinking we had a bad connection, we hung up and called back. About the time we heard him say, "fire", we saw smoke billowing from the direction of our home—the home where all our memories were kept; the home where we had raised our children!

It is hard to describe the feelings you have standing and watching your home burn. At that moment, life had turned surreal. Time seemed to stand still... and rush by. Ultimately, the house was destroyed by the fire, smoke, and water.

Praise God, Sarah was off at college!

Praise God, Matthew got out alive and physically unharmed!

Praise God, we had not been asleep when the fire started!

The Lord Jesus is truly our Savior!

Friends and neighbors came with comfort and aid—instruments of the Holy Spirit, our Comforter and Helper. Somehow, they understood what we really needed. Praise God, He brings peace in the midst of chaos! And then He showed up in a supernatural way.

Somewhere in the midst of this "tragedy-in-progress", God whispered into our hearts, "I am sovereign. Nothing happens outside of my will. I am a good God, I love you, and I have a plan for you. Reckon it in your hearts." And so we did; and we continued to remind each other to reckon it as true. He also told us to grieve the loss. At the time, we did not understand the importance of this step, but by His grace we obeyed. It was a decisive act. Praise God for His rhema (right now) word!

The Pivotal Moment

As Beth and I "settled" into our first temporary quarters (the Holiday Inn Express), we turned to our Heavenly Father in prayer. Beth began, "Father God, whatever you have for us in this, we receive it."

This was the surrender He was looking for—it opened up the storehouse of Heaven. With one word (our "whatever"), we had entered into the purpose of Almighty God. Our tragedy immediately became an adventure. Praise God for His encouragement in the prayers of a godly wife!

Comfort and Aid

As we mentioned, many neighbors and friends reached out with comfort and aid. Neighbors we had never met and friends who just "happened to be driving by." From the firefighters to the Red Cross, God's grace was poured out on us in a tremendous way—the first evidence of His extravagant love. And it didn't stop on the night of the fire: Gift cards for Matthew from his friends and the faculty of Heirway Christian School; clothes, soap, deodorant, meals, and cold hard cash from Beth's friends in the Douglas County School System; and meals from our family at New River Community

Church. Praise God, His encouragement that everything was going to be all right was just, well, supernatural!

The Evidence of God's Orchestration

Before continuing, it's only fair to warn the reader that the following is filled with seemingly small and inconsequential facts. We capture them here as evidence of God's careful and exquisite orchestration. Perhaps they are only understood by those who have been through similar journeys. We pray this testimony will help others recognize when God is doing the same for them (orchestrating). It will make the adventure more exciting, and less fearful. Praise God, His eye is on the sparrow and He does know the number of hairs on our heads!

The first bit of orchestration came via a phone call from some friends at church. Their neighbors were currently on an extended mission assignment in New Orleans—helping to direct the clean-up from Hurricane Katrina—and were willing to let us use their home. Within two days we were out of the hotel and into a comfortable home. Praise God, He allowed us to be a part of His working all things to the good of those who love Him, and are called to His purpose!

Being blessed with a comfortable home gave us time to address some important issues. One of those was replacing our truck, which had been fuel for the fire. We can't explain it—and, as we mentioned earlier, we didn't deserve it—but the Lord saw fit to provide a 2003 Nissan Frontier for approximately half its estimated cost.

And as if that wasn't enough of an "I've got you covered" from the Lord, there was the "Overlook at Riverpointe" blessing. You see, we really needed a place to live closer to Matthew's school, and our burned house. Had we been in a hurry, we would not have experienced the connection God made between one of Beth's coworkers and the builder who had just finished their new home. Long story short, we were able to move into a brand new house within a few miles of our burned one.

We were graced with the wisdom and provision to have insurance that would pay for this temporary housing and the furniture that provided comfortable living conditions. Contrary to the stories we had heard, we were having a gift of God experience with our insurance company. We have never heard of anyone having the supernatural favor we had with them.

And now our eyes were wide open to God's adventure. We began looking for ways to share what the Lord was doing. It was at this time He gave the "Chaos Navigation" teaching. He also allowed us to minister encouragement into many people's lives. For example, our new builder-landlord was having a very difficult time getting along with, and receiving payment from, one of his customers. The Lord led me to pray the supernatural peace and joy in his heart would so impact his customer that the relationship would completely change. Guess what? The customer caught up on his payments and even went so far as to praise him for his work.

God's orchestration is truly amazing—not only in the day-to-day, but over the long term. Has there ever been a time when the existing house market was so much more attractive than the build-new market? Consequently, the reconstruction cost of our existing home was so high the Insurance Adjuster allowed us to begin shopping around for something we could move into immediately. Talk about the Lord giving you the desires of your heart! This was exactly what we needed.

The search for a new home began with another unusual circumstance. Beth tried to call an agent who was listed on a house we were interested in. However, it was the weekend and we had to "settle for" the realtor on call. Reluctantly, we agreed to meet with him. We soon discovered God had provided us with the most professional and selfless Realtor we had ever met. Imagine that!

The realtor first showed us a house in Chestatee Farms—a foreclosure that would have normally been out of our price range. It was a museum of a house, big enough for two or three families, on four acres of land. It didn't feel like "home", but we felt encouraged by the Lord to pursue it. In the process, the insurance adjuster agreed to commit another $15,000 to fix any damage to this or any other property we bought. And so, with what we were allotted by the adjuster, we submitted what would be one of three bids being considered by the fore-closure management company. A decision would come in four days.

God Speaks Again

Early in the morning on the day we were to find out about the Chestatee Farms "museum", the Lord awakened me to come meet Him in prayer. The moment my knees hit the floor, the Lord said, "I am not going to give you the house. I am going to give you more. But you will have to trust Me with this one." And so, we were very excited (and not at all surprised) to hear we lost the bid. But what was the "more" about? How was that possible?

The Lord encouraged me the "trust me with this one" meant letting go of finding a home with acreage (like we had with our burned house). This freed us to begin looking at homes in subdivisions. Our realtor was very patient with us in this change of direction, but probably a bit confused and concerned with our insistence on looking at "more" sized properties (we weren't brave enough to tell him about the "more" message).

Our Failing Patience

If it was going to happen, we wanted to get into a new home before Beth started back to work. But things weren't working out like we expected. One offer after another was refused.

We placed a bid on a beautiful property in the Riverwalk Subdivision. Beth loved it, but the owners flat out refused our bid; even calling us (outside of protocol) to tell us they just couldn't accept such a disparate offer. Time was running out. As the weeks went by, we became more doubtful about the "more" message.

It was now July, and we were getting antsy. To be transparently honest, gone was the "more" adventure, replaced by a desperate search for something "acceptable". Oh, how quickly we can lose focus on, and trust in, the Faithful One.

And so, with our impatience getting the best of us, we placed a bid on a foreclosed house we felt could be upgraded to meet our needs. Our realtor called the next day with the news our bid had been accepted. But there was something more—praise God for on-time surprises!

Our Impatience Meets God's Perfect Timing

When God brings an adventure to its closure, He often does so quickly—so quick it takes your breath away. We didn't know it at the time, but He was working the timing out so we would know it was all in His hands—even in our moment of doubt and self-decision.

When our realtor said, "Your bid has been accepted, but something very strange has happened", my heart jumped. It was electric, like God had dropped in an anticipation and an answer at the same time. "The owners of the Riverwalk house have changed their minds and would like to sell you the house (for the amount we offered), if you are still interested." Were we still interested? It was all I could do not to throw down the phone and run around the room, hoopin' and hollerin' (I did that later).

Beth and Sarah were out shopping when I called them. If I had known they were in the car, I would have waited. It's a wonder they didn't dance the car right off the road. Praise God for His extravagant joy!

The Sum of God's Blessing (So Far)

At the closing, the owners told us they had been puzzled and frustrated that their beautiful home had not sold for more than two years; and then they said, "Now we know He was holding it for you." Praise God for His divine orchestration! They even came over to the house to show us how things worked and how they had decorated it. They left after praying a blessing over our new home and our family. Praise God for the Body of Christ!

As you can see, the sum of God's blessing in this adventure cannot be measured in dollars, square footage, etc. But God has blessed us in practical ways we would like to recognize:

1. He moved us into a house that is twice the size of our burned home—still with nothing owed (we were out of debt before the fire);

2. He provided an additional $15,000 for repairs—a house without maintenance for two years needs more repairs than you might think;

3. He razed and removed our burned house—though it's still weird to think our home and belongings are buried somewhere; and,

4. He left us with the 7.8 acres we had with our burned home—His response to Rob's trust; and the over-the-top evidence of His extravagant love!

We believe the blessings of this adventure are not over for us, and for those our new home will be used to bless. We are holding this gift loosely, because we know it is God's possession. We ask that you pray for us to be good stewards with our new home.

Epilogue

Ironically, this tragedy has also been used by God to bring healing. The last three years have been challenging for us. At times we have felt torn apart by circumstances, fears, and disappointments. But God has used this "tragedy-turned-adventure" to bring us together—in the shadow of His extravagant love. Could that be God's intention in every tribulation? That has truly been our experience. It is the "God working all things to the good of those that love Him and are called to His purpose."

We pray that in all things, you will also know the love, grace and power God desires to manifest in your lives.

In His Abounding Grace,

Rob, Beth, Sarah, and Matthew

Disciplines for the Process of Faith

The Foundational Disciplines

A house built on a poor foundation will not endure through the difficult seasons (Matthew 7:24-25). Appropriating the grace of God for the fullness of faith requires a strong foundation throughout the process. Hearing the sayings of Jesus and doing them is the wise man's approach for building strong foundations. Consequently, the foundational disciplines of the faith process embrace four of Jesus' most empowering directives. Each one is fundamental to the Christian faith. One might argue neglect in either of them is both disobedience and dangerous to the journey.

Waiting in Prayer – Prayer is essential because faith comes by hearing and hearing by the word of God (Romans 10:17). We are referring to listening-prayer in the closet and in community; prayer that expects to hear God speak and is consequently hungry to know His voice. Seriously, if communicating with Almighty God is not a strong enough motivation for the sacrifice of our temporal activities and/or sleep, what then will persuade us?

Bible Study – *All Scripture is given by inspiration of God, and is profitable for doctrine, for reproof, for correction, for instruction in righteousness, that the man of God may be complete, thoroughly equipped for every good work (2 Timothy 3:16-17).* Bible reading plans often inhibit our understanding of God and His purposes for our life. Reading is the means, not the end. The Holy Spirit must be allowed, even encouraged, to guide us into the truth of Scripture and its intention for our faith. We must be attentive to the one verse or phrase that will hold our attention for days or weeks.

Loving God and Man – The Great Commandments (Mark 12:33) should be more to us than beloved passages for memorization and mental assent. They should be more than demands we try to obey. Loving God and our fellow man should be our life! Indeed, it is either life or law. Love that is obeyed as law only leads to death (2 Corinthians 3:6). Ironically, quite the opposite is also true: a life of love empowers the children of God to fulfill the law (Romans 8:4).

Being Made to Make Disciples – Moving from the Great Commandments to the Great Commission (Matthew 28:18-20), we discover a discipline lost to much of the church. For many, unlearning the world's ways is a critical part of this discipline. Hearing is needed. Even more so is the doing, actually making disciples (versus converts). This discipline is strongly related to our obedience to the faith. After all, the One Who has been given all authority in heaven and on earth, our Master, Captain, and King, has commissioned us all.

The foundational disciplines are like military infrastructure (e.g., communications, supply lines, enemy intelligence, and coordinated engagement). We will not overcome our carnal mind—our number one enemy—without them. Exercising these disciplines empowers us to inflict our enemy with spiritual shock and awe. The resulting position of strength enables and encourages us to press the attack.

Disciplines for the Hearing of Faith

This matter of hearing God has become much more controversial and confusing than it needs to be. With all due respect and love for all who are called by God to teach, it is simply ridiculous to think God no longer speaks. The Father loves sharing right-now wisdom and revelation with His children. He is our loving Father; why would He limit Himself in this way. The Greek word *rhema*, found in Romans 10:17 means "that which is spoken (Vine, Unger, & White, 1965)."

> **Surrender** – Surrender is not something we normally think about as a discipline. It is likely true, and regrettable, that we do not think about surrender much at all. For Christians in the West, surrender is difficult because it flies in the face of our culture. Countries are great because their people refuse to surrender. To surrender would be a disgrace. Backing down is for cowards. Of course, this is not what the Scriptures tell us (John 5:30). Surrender is the absolute first step into the kingdom of God. Let that sink in. Much of humility is dependent on surrender, including Jesus' humility in coming to dwell among us. An intentional and decisive surrender is the first step in hearing the word of God.

> **Worship** – Generally speaking, the church has succumbed to two debilitating errors regarding worship. First, we have fallen into the event trap, that worship is something we do at a particular time and place. Most will agree and pray that worship is meant to be something more (Psalm 100:4). We must, however, resist the temptation to agree and move on. It will do us good to consider the contrast between our assumed understanding and our actions.

Our second debilitating error is our improperly or poorly focused attention. As congregations and media outlets become increasingly competitive for a share of the Christian market, worship has lost its intended focus. The worship experience has been compromised by the perceived need to entertain. Worship entertainment has become the draw. Consequently, most Christians are being discipled to pursue worship for their personal benefit.

Quiet – Quieting the mind is perhaps the greatest challenge to our hearing the word of God. The world and our life choices have given us much to think about. Adopting a simpler life would help tremendously in this regard. That is beyond the scope of this study, but we strongly suggest its pursuit just the same. In the meantime, God has given us the method by which we may quiet our minds. We are to take every thought captive to the obedience of Christ (2 Corinthians 10:5). While this is perhaps easier said (or written) than done, it is not a complicated practice. I can personally testify to God's blessing in its exercise.

Desire – The purposes of God for every season of our lives are found in the desires He has placed in our hearts. He intends to give these desires to us (Psalm 37:4). Consequently, He speaks with us about them and uses them to motivate our continuing response. It is therefore reasonable to assume He expects us to discover and maintain our attention to them in our conversations with Him. We must be keen to cull out those desires that have been deposited in our heart and mind by Satan, the world and our flesh. The more completely we reject them, the less distracting they will be—leaving us to hear what God has to say about the desires He shares with us.

These are the four disciplines that have served me best in hearing the word of God. We humbly share them, recognizing there are others which supplement and build on these. In fact, God has recently brought "waiting on Him" to my attention. We will leave it to the reader to search that one out. Andrew Murray's book, *Waiting on God* (2017), is a great starting point.

Disciplines for Obedience to the Faith

Obedience is both doing what one knows to be right and not doing what is wrong. Here, we are primarily dealing with the former. However, God might just as well say, "stop doing that," in which case, "not doing" requires the same obedience to the faith. In either case, obedience to the faith is the bridge between the hearing of faith and the work of faith. It serves to move faith from our heart to our feet, hands, and mouth. For that to happen, our mind and brain must be engaged and disciplined. Consequently, the battle with our carnal mind is most intense in this phase of the process. Forewarned is forearmed. Be strong in the Lord, and in the power of His might (Ephesians 6:10). Our Captain has given us these disciplines as weaponry for the battle.

> **Repent** – The results of true repentance are sorrowfulness, turning from sin, change in behavior, the proverbial "about face." These all begin with "to change one's mind for the better", the literal meaning of the Greek word *metanoeō* (from *Thayer's Greek Lexicon*, found on www.BlueLetterBible.com). Don't miss this: repentance begins with a change of our mind. This is true for the initial repentance that leads to salvation and

every repentance that follows (Acts 2:38). The process of faith includes an iterative changing of our minds.

Reckon – As the truth of God presents itself, we must reckon with it. Translated from the Greek word *logizomai,* reckon means to account the truth of God to be our truth (like balancing an accounting ledger). Paul encourages us to reckon ourselves dead to sin and alive to God, in Christ Jesus (Romans 6:11). *Logizomai* is also translated "consider" (Romans 8:18), "thought" (1 Corinthians 13:11), and "meditate" (Philippians 4:8).

Renew – In His wisdom, God decided to give us a new heart, but not a new mind (Ezekiel 36:25-27). We have the mind of Christ (1 Corinthians 2:16), but exercising it, by all indications, is difficult at best. Consequently, our minds must be renewed, a significant part of our transformation (Romans 12:2). Renew (*anakainoō*) means *"to cause to grow up, to make new (as in renovation), to be changed into a new kind of life as opposed to the former corrupt state."* Taken from Blue Letter Bible's Outline of Biblical Usage (2019), this definition suggests our maturity as Christians is dependent on the renewing of our minds. 2 Corinthians 4:16, Ephesians 4:23, and Colossians 3:10 are additionally helpful references.

Submit – As we prepare for the work of faith, the practice of submission becomes important in two additional ways. First, there is manifestation of the fruit of the Spirit (Galatians 5:21-23). Our submission begins with a desire to bear the Spirit's fruit for the glory of our Father in heaven (John 15:8). Secondly, we must submit to the Spirit's gifts (1 Corinthians 12:1-11), beginning with a resolution and conviction that we have no preference, that we desire the one(s) He wants to manifest through us.

One of the more obvious and important revelations here is our dependence on the Holy Spirit in the exercise of these disciplines. This explains a lot, for many Christians have grown up with little teaching about the Holy Spirit's person and work. For those of you who share this history with me, Billy Graham's *The Holy Spirit* (2000), as well as *The Word and Power Church* by Doug Banister (1999), are two excellent resources. You will be truly amazed at the Holy Spirit's role and responsibility for our faith journey.

Disciplines for the Work of Faith

Discussing faith and works together has become a difficult, anxiety-inducing exercise for most of the Body of Christ. This is not so much due to an identifiable point of disagreement as to the subconscious suspicion that what the other believes may be different and/or a challenge to something we have been taught. This again is a ploy of our carnal mind to protect closely held convictions and opinions and to maintain control and comfort.

For convenience's sake, here is a summary of God's intention for the interplay and dependence of grace, faith, and works.

Grace, faith, and works cannot be understood apart from each other. Our faith, which is a gift of God—appropriates the grace of God. The grace of God manifests itself in His good works. His good works perfect (i.e., complete) our faith as we walk in them. Faith without these works is dead (i.e., without effect).

Because these works are His, we have no claim of credit for them (i.e., they are not our work unto salvation).

God's grace is the source and strength of His good work for both salvation and the ongoing good work He does in and through us (Philippians 2:13). When the Scriptures speak of "your good works" (as in Matthew 5:16), they are speaking of the good works God is doing. We are instruments only. His good works are, therefore, justifiably for His name, kingdom, and glory.

Work done without faith is also dead—dead works (Romans 14:23). It is possible to do great works that are dead to Jesus Christ (Matthew 7:21-23). The only way to ensure the works in which we are walking are good is to know they are God's. We must know His voice and obey when we hear Him. As previously argued, this level of intimacy is a critical success factor for our salvation, for the perfecting of our faith, and for reaching our potential as His workmanship.

The work of faith, by the grace of God at work in and through us, is described in Ephesians 3:20 as exceedingly abundantly above all we can ask or think. Recognizing that nothing is impossible for Him, consider that the "exceedingly abundantly above all" is "according to the power that works in us." The power that works in us is His working to will and to do for His good pleasure (Philippians 2:13).

And so, we come to four disciplines for the work of faith.

Trust – Trust is the door between obedience to the faith and the work of faith (Psalm 37:5-6). One cannot trust the LORD while trusting the carnal mind; they are at enmity with one another. Furthermore, the carnal mind draws most of its strength from our trust. Consequently, the development of this discipline is both critical and greatly opposed. We must recognize, but not be fearful of the fact that the carnal mind allies itself with Satan and the world. Satan repeats the same old lie, "You cannot trust Him. You should be your own god." The world vigorously waves its hand, eagerly volunteering as a suitable substitute for our hope, security, and power. Our carnal mind plays along, desiring to maintain some level of control. This, of course, must be resisted.

Practice – I admire people who are natural risk takers. They have an advantage when it comes to the work of faith. They do not have that built-in streak of caution like so many of us conservative folk. They go with their gut (i.e., not with their head). In many respects, this is the crux of our dilemma. In this age of reason, the head has gotten in the way of the heart. Our thinking it through has mucked up the works. It is time for most of us to just believe, trust, and step into the work of faith (1 John 3:7).

Fast – In the Old and New Testament, to fast means to do without food and drink for a day, or from customary and choice nourishment for a longer span of time. God has made it clear, through the prophet Isaiah (Chapter 58), that fasting has been prescribed for specific spiritual and physical outcomes, and these are predominately not for ourselves. Furthermore, fasting teaches us that sacrifice has its rewards. It is hard to imagine a greater lesson for today's Christian—a much needed defense against the consumerism of Western society that severely threatens the church.

Fellowship – The desire to be alone is not a desire God has placed in our hearts. He does not make, nor does He regularly use, "loners." The New Testament consistently encourages our desire for fellowship. Being in fellowship and gathering with a crowd are not the same. Fellowship in the kingdom of God is marked by our being unified unto the measure of the stature of the fullness of Christ (Ephesians 4:13). We are to be as much members of one another as the Father and Son (Romans 12:5). Granted, this is beyond our ability, even our imagination. It is for this very reason we are encouraged to steadfastly participate in Jesus Christ's work to build His church.

The work of the faith is not possible without the hearing of faith and obedience to the faith. Conversely, the process of faith is ineffectual without the corresponding work. This leads to two concluding thoughts:

1. Disciplines are something we do. They are not mental assents, attitudes, nor character traits. Hopes and dreams are insufficient. All of the disciplines require action.
2. Many of the disciplines work together. For example, the truths born out of repentance must be reckoned as our own, a means of participating with the Holy Spirit's efforts to renew our mind.

Let us conclude by reemphasizing our insufficiency to practice the disciplines of faith (2 Corinthians 3:5). Without the sufficient grace of God (2 Corinthians 12:9), the disciplines would be impossible to sustain, and ineffectual in their exercise. We would become discouraged without the encouragement of the Father. If Jesus is not making us, then we will soon grow proud of our progress. We will be lost in our search for the truth without our guide, the Holy Spirit.

God bless you with listening ears and obedient hearts. Let the adventure begin!

Discovering Your Sphere of Influence

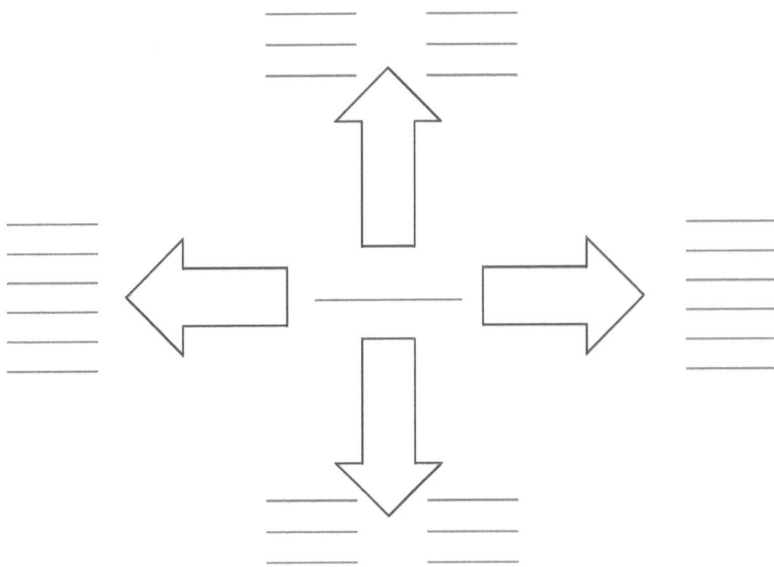

This is a tool to assist in your hearing from the Lord regarding the spheres of influence and relationships He has established for you to weather the storms and navigate the chaos.

1. Prayerfully and intentionally surrender to the Lord's reign and direction. (Father God, I surrender my heart to Your reign. I lay aside my agendas and expectations. My desire is to hear Your voice, that I would know You and the desires You have for me.)

2. Put your name on the center line. (Father, here I am. I am Your child, eager to be used by You as a strong house in my spheres of influence.)

3. In the arrows, write the names of the places where you spend the most time. Write in additional arrows as necessary, but be sensitive to the Holy Spirit highlighting one or two. (Father, You know my comings and goings. You have orchestrated my life to put me

in these places for Your glory and the advancement of Your kingdom. Which are the most important to You for this season of my life?)

4. On the lines at the end of the arrows, put the names of the people with whom you spend the most time. Listen closely to the Holy Spirit emphasizing one or more of them. (Father, who are the people in this sphere of influence You are most interested in discipling through me?)

5. Keep this in a place where you see it once or twice a day. It will remind you God has a purpose for you in these spheres of influence. Use the names listed as subjects of prayer—that God would prepare both you and them for a divine exchange of encouragement and edification.

6. Periodically, review this guide with God, asking Him to further align it with His will.

7. Share this tool with those you are discipling. If you are not making disciples who are making disciples, then you are not making disciples.

Bibliography

Banister, D. (1999). *The Word and Power Church*. Grand Rapids, MI: Zondervan Publishing House.

Cahn, J.; *The Harbinger;* Lake Mary, FL; Frontline

Chambers, O. (1992). *My Utmost for His Highest*. Grand Rapids, MI: Discovery House.

Crabb, L. (2006). *The PAPA Prayer*. Brentwood, TN: Integrity Publishers.

Graham, B. (1988). *The Holy Spirit*; Nashville, TN: Thomas Nelson Publishing.

Murray, A. (2014). *Waiting on God*. Apollo, PA: Ichthus Publications.

Roberts, F. (1973). *Come Away My Beloved*. Uhrichsville, OH: Barbour Books.

Streetman, R. (2020). *An Enemy Lies Within*. Hoover, AL: Archdeacon Books.

Streetman, R. (2015). *A Storm is Coming* [Kindle version]. Retrieved from https://www.smashwords.com/books/view/585431.

Streetman, R. (2014). *The Map Maker*. Atlanta, GA: Mindshift Publishing.

Tozer, A. W. (2015). *God's Pursuit of Man*. Chicago, IL: Moody Publishers.

Tozer, A. W. (1991). *The Price of Neglect and Other Essays*. Camp Hill, PA: Christian Publications.

Unknown. (2021). *Outline of Biblical Usage*. Retrieved from http://www.blueletterbible.org/.

Vine, W. E., Merrill, F. U., & White, W. (1985). *Vine's Complete Expository Dictionary of Old and New Testament Words*. Nashville, TN: Thomas Nelson Publishers.

Recommended Reading

General

Studies in the Sermon on the Mount;
D. Martyn Lloyd-Jones

The Benedict Option; Rod Dreher

The Normal Christian Life; Watchman Nee

The Storm Before the Calm; George Friedman

Section One—Inspect

An Enemy Lies Within; Rob Streetman

The Christian Mind; Harry Blamires

The Treasure Principle; Randy Alcorn

Section Two—Restore

Life in the Spirit; A. W. Tozer

The Map Maker; Rob Streetman

The PAPA Prayer; Larry Crabb

Section Three—Restore

Abiding in Christ; Andrew Murray

Prepare; J. Paul Nyquist

Radical; David Platt

Christian Disciplines

Conformed to His Image; Kenneth Boa

The Spirit of the Disciplines; Dallas Willard

Waiting on God; Andrew Murray

About the Author

R ob is the President and Founder of inLight Consulting, Inc., a not-for-profit ministry dedicated to encouraging, edifying, and equipping workplace leaders to become disciple makers and transformation agents in their spheres of influence.

Rob spent more than twenty-five years in the Information Technology field of the Financial Services Industry, where he served in various leadership roles and participated in many organization transformation efforts as an Enterprise Architect. At the Lord's insistence, Rob retired from IT to serve Him in full-time ministry.

God has used Rob as His pen to write four books: *The Map Maker, The Map Maker's Guide, A Storm is Coming,* and *An Enemy Lies Within.* Together, they have also written hundreds of articles for *The inLight Adventure Blog* (with distribution in several media outlets), all for the transformation of workplace leaders into disciple makers and transformation agents.

Rob and his wife Beth live in Douglas County, Georgia. They have two adult children. Rob's hobbies include reading, cycling, hiking, and otherwise discovering more of the Lord's creation.

Discover Other Titles

Rob Streetman has given us a fresh way to understand the call of God through creative use of a parable. *The Map Maker* has been created to help Christian Leaders enjoy the adventure God has for them. Along the way, there will be a mixture of excitement and fear. You will find yourself identifying with Somebody's struggle, and encouraged by revelations and breakthroughs as he navigates through often-difficult terrain on his journey of faith. *The Map Maker* will lead you on a treasure hunt to search out the mysteries of the kingdom of God. You will discover the reward to be well worth the effort.

As a teaching complement to *The Map Maker*, *The Map Maker's Guide* provides a comprehensive guide for the Workplace Leader who desires to make disciples and transform their spheres of influence. The Guide consists of twenty-six turn-key lessons that can be taught in one-hour sessions. Each lesson contains everything the leader needs to disciple others into joyful, Spirit-filled ministry in the Workplace: a spiritual exercise, word definitions, the core lesson, assignments, and a complementary devotion.

In 2015, Jonathan Cahn wrote a book (*The Harbinger*) that prophesied a coming storm for America. Many began to prepare—in a physical sense. We discerned a deeper, spiritual warning, and decided to write a series of articles regarding God's warning, not to America, but to the church that resides here. God allows and creates storms to test and refine. Our hope is that many will become houses with strong foundations and that those who have lost theirs will find refuge.

Christians have turned to their carnal mind as a trusted advisor. We must seriously and soberly consider the way we think as Christians. The carnal mind—forever at enmity with God—has wreaked havoc on the Western church, leaving us in desperate need of a reformation. Where do reformations begin if not with repentance? As the reader will discover, true repentance begins with a change of the mind. *An Enemy Lies Within* exposes the carnal mind as the #1 enemy of God and His children, explores the process He has provided for overcoming our carnal mind's deceptions, and encourages and equips overcomers in the liberation of others.

Connect with the Author

Follow us on Twitter:
twitter.com/RobStreetman

Connect with us on LinkedIn:
www.linkedin.com/pub/rob-streetman/1b/477/1a5

Friend us on Facebook:
www.facebook.com/rob.streetman.7

Like inLight Consulting on Facebook:
https://www.facebook.com/
Inlight-Consulting-414307808658950/

Subscribe to the inLight Adventure Blog:
Send request to rob@inlightconsulting.com

Receive our Newsletter:
Send request to rob@inlightconsulting.com

Favorite us at Smashwords:
www.smashwords.com/profile/view/RobStreetman